STEPHEN TURNBULL

SAMURAI WARRIORS

ILLUSTRATIONS BY JAMES FIELD

PHOTOGRAPHS BY STEPHEN TURNBULL

BLANDFORD

This paperback first published 1991
Hardback first published in the UK 1987 by Blandford Press
an imprint of Cassell plc
Villiers House, 41-47 Strand, London WC2N 5JE

Reprinted October 1987
Reprinted June 1988

Distributed in the United States by
Sterling Publishing Co Inc
387 Park Avenue South, New York, NY 10016

Distributed in Australia by
Capricorn Link (Australia) Pty Ltd
PO Box 665, Lane Cove, NSW 2066

British Library Cataloguing in Publication Data
Turnbull, SR
    Samurai warriors
    1. Samurai-History
    1. Title
    305.5′2   DS827.S3

ISBN 0 7137 1767 X hardback
ISBN 0 7137 2285 1 paperback

Typeset by Best-Set Typesetter Ltd, Hong Kong
Printed in Singapore by Kyodo Printing Co (S'pore) Pte Ltd

SAMURAI WARRIORS

To the author's mother, Joyce M. Turnbull,
and the artist's wife, Sally Field

Contents

Acknowledgements

Until the publication of this book, non-Japanese-speaking readers have been denied an authoritative account of the development of the costume and equipment of the Japanese samurai as it relates to changes in military history, such as has been produced by scholars like Yoshihiko Sasama. Several of Sasama's indispensable works, especially his *Zukai Nihon Katchu Jiten* (1973), and *Zuroku Nihon no Katchu Bugu Jiten* (1981) have been consulted initially on points of detail for this work, but in every case the resulting illustration or description has been taken from source, making *Samurai Warriors* totally original. It draws upon 20 years of research into samurai history, armour and weapons and, using exclusively Japanese sources, paints a picture of the samurai in words, photographs and via specially commissioned artwork that is unique outside Japan itself.

Such use of rare materials could not have been entertained without the help and support of many individuals and organisations. In this context particular mention must be made of Mrs Nahoko Kitajima of Moriguchi City, Osaka, and her colleague Mr Nishikawa; and also Mr Yukito Kaiki and Miss Nobuyo Ichifugi, of Kanazawa. Much valuable information was also supplied by the helpful staff of the Tokyo Offices of the Prefectures of Yamanashi, Shizuoka, Gifu, Shiba, Ishikawa and Aichi. Museums and collections that opened their doors to us include the Nagashino Castle Preservation Hall, the Minatogawa Shrine Museum, Kobe, the Ieyasukan at Okazaki, the Gifu City Historical Museum, the Sanada Museum, Matsushiro, Ueda Castle Museum, Osaka Castle Museum, Hamamatsu Castle Museum, the Nampian Kannon-ji at Kawachi-Nagano, the Memorial Hall at Nakamura Park, Nagoya, and the Takeda Museum at the Erinji, Enzan, in addition to well-known national collections such as the Tokyo National Museum.

This book is the product of a partnership. Quite the most enjoyable and rewarding aspect of its production has been to place my research beside the considerable artistic talents of James Field. It has proved to be a fruitful co-operation, and I know James joins with me in saying the biggest 'thank-you' to our wives, Jo Turnbull and Sally Field, without whose happy tolerance none of what follows would have been possible.

Stephen Turnbull

8

1

Heian Period

The samurai were the knights of Medieval Japan. Like their counterparts in Europe, they began as a military élite and became a social élite, their prize being the triumph which their swords had won for them. The history of the samurai is very much the history of Japan itself, so for convenience we will follow a chronological sequence based on the traditional divisions of the Japanese historical eras. The 'Heian Period' (during which the word 'samurai' is first used) derives from the name by which the capital city, Kyoto, was known at the time: 'Heian-kyo' or the city of heavenly peace.

The Early Warriors

There is no doubt as to when the samurai officially ceased to exist as a separate class. The decisive date must be 1876, when the wearing of swords was forbidden to all except the national conscript army of the new Japan. What is at issue is how the samurai began. Exactly how did a military élite emerge? This is a problem of Japanese history that has still not been adequately explained. In terms of the long history of the Japanese people the samurai are comparative newcomers. The word itself hardly pre-dates the eleventh century AD and follows a millennium of years of war. *Samurai* means, literally, 'those who serve', implying the rendering of honourable military service by an élite to an overlord, which is effectually what the samurai existed to provide until the time when the class was abolished in the 1870s. These three factors: military prowess, élitism and service to another, are the keys to identifying the origin of the samurai.

Ancient records give us some clues as to the samurai antecedents. Within the *Nihongi*, the *Chronicles of Japan*, compiled sometime during the first decades of the eighth century AD, may be found the term *bugei*, or 'martial arts', so no doubt some degree of military specialism existed in the armies of the period, whether they were under the control of the central government or local officials. The early history of Japan was as much a time of conflict as any of the 'samurai centuries' that followed.

In the year AD 672 we are given a hint of one role which the future samurai were to make very much their own, that of the mounted archer, a form of warfare, which, it would appear, was already achieving an élite status. In AD 671 the Emperor Tenchi died, his death causing one of those succession disputes with which samurai history is littered. Emperor Tenchi had apparently promised the throne to his brother, who had declined the honour and subsequently become a monk, so that on Tenchi's death his son ascended to the throne. This was, however, only within a month of the uncle renouncing the world, and the opportunity to take up that which he had recently discarded must have proved very tempting. As a result the brother left the monastery and revolted against his nephew. What is interesting from a military point of view is that he made good use of the rapid striking power of a force of mounted archers. The coup was successful, and he ascended the throne as Emperor Temmu. The accounts of Temmu's coup, and the achievements of his reign, come from the above-mentioned *Nihongi*, which was compiled under the jurisdiction of Temmu's daughter, so its claims for Temmu's military accomplishments may have to be regarded with some scepticism. Nevertheless, this is the first written account of the mounted archer in action, a model of military accomplishment that was to be the mark of the élite samurai.

Rivalry such as this between Imperial princes was far less common as a reason for war than the continuing need for campaigns against the aboriginal inhabitants of the Japanese islands, the Ainu. The old accounts make it quite clear that the suppression of these people was seen almost as a moral duty and an act of spreading civilisation, as it is referred to in the *Chronicles* as *emishi no seiobatsu* or 'punishment of the emishi'. *Emishi*, which

---

PLATE 1   *A samurai of the time of the Later Three Years' War*

In contradiction to its title, this war lasted from 1083 to 1087, and was one of the several 'little wars' in which the Minamoto clan rose to prominence by defeating rebels.

The samurai wears a suit of armour of the classic *yoroi* style, laced with thick silken cords. The *yoroi* is the typical samurai armour of the time and is derived from Asiatic styles of lamellar armour, whereby an armour plate is made up of several small plates fastened together in some way, rather than using single large plates of metal or leather. The plate of a *yoroi* would be made by binding a row of scales together with leather thongs, then lacquering the whole to make a waterproof, light and tough protection. A number of these plates would then be fastened together by cords, overlapping slightly in concertina fashion. The *yoroi* is the style which we will meet time and time again as we go through samurai

history. The box-like body-armour, or *do*, hangs from the shoulders and is fastened around the waist. Only the plate under the right arm is separate. There is a leather covering, beautifully patterned, on the front of the armour, called the *tsurubashiri*, which gives the appearance of a breastplate. The two appendages, called the *sendan-no-ita* and the *kyubi-no-ita*, which hang in front, are designed to protect the cords holding the armour from severance by swordstrokes.

For an indication of what this armour would look like from the rear, consult the illustration on p. 20.

The helmet worn with a *yoroi* was made from a number of iron plates riveted together. We can see the large rivet heads left protruding from the helmet surface, in the style known as a *hoshi-kabuto*. His hair has been gathered into a pigtail on top of his head inside an *eboshi* cap, which protrudes through the *tehen*, the

hole formed where the ends of the helmet plates meet, thus providing a padding for the weight of the helmet. He wears a *kote*, or armoured sleeve, on his left arm only, thus leaving the right freer for drawing a bow, for at this period in Japanese history the samurai was essentially a mounted archer. His sword is suspended from a belt beside a *tanto*, or dagger.

The figure is based on an illustration in the *Gosannen no eki emaki* (Scroll of the Later Three Years' War) in Tokyo National Museum, with additional details of the armour being taken from a *yoroi* of the period preserved in the Oyamazumi Shrine Museum, Omishima (Hiroshima Prefecture). The common soldier beside him has much simpler armour called *do-maru*, or 'body-wrappers', made of similar lamellar construction.

A map showing the general outline of Japan and its main islands, and also its position in relation to the Asiatic mainland.

is probably a variant of the Ainu word for 'man', was used in the sense of 'barbarian', implying the disdain of a civilised state, much as the word was used by the Romans against the Celtic tribes of Europe. *Emishi* was actually the politest term their enemies used for them, as the indigenous population are elsewhere variously referred to as 'earth spiders'.

The *emishi* proved to be stubborn fighters and early Emperors very soon made a habit of recruiting pacified *emishi* for their armies, a practice that had on occasions already been adopted by rebels against the throne, for whom these discontented and rebellious people were an obvious source of

Prince Yamato-Takeru, slayer of serpents and semi-mythological hero of early Japan. Yamato's career, as the brave individual warrior, sets the tone for the most cherished ideals of the samurai. His statue is in the Kenroku-en Gardens, Kanazawa.

support. They proved to be worthy of their hire, and many of the military traditions which later became associated with the samurai had their origins in these warriors. Even the curved sword, so much a symbol of the samurai, probably owes its origin to the weapons carried by *emishi* who were recruited as guards for the Imperial Court in the latter part of the ninth century. But, most important of all, it was the *emishi* campaigns, which were fought against soldiers who were familiar with their territory, that provided the practice for the wars of later years when the samurai would take on their own kind in struggles for the fertile lands of Japan.

For an explanation of the élite nature of the samurai we must look elsewhere than the barbarian *emishi*. There was a clearly defined tendency for certain families to acquire reputations for military excellence from the earliest centuries. Examples are the Otomo in the eighth century, who held the post of hereditary palace guards, and the Sakanoue in the ninth, but it is not until the tenth century that we see the emergence of 'warrior houses' of samurai. The formation of these units, based on the possession of land rather than patronage, was the most important social development during these early years. Typically, such a unit would be based around a central familial core, often with aristocratic connections. In many cases there was an actual lineage from a scion of the Imperial House, an honoured ancestor who had left Kyoto for the distant provinces to open up new rice-lands, pacify barbarians, and generally make a name for himself. The members were bound together by ties of loyalty and reward. These 'warrior houses', or 'clans' (either translation gives the reader a good mental picture of their fundamental nature), prospered best in areas remote from the capital, where they were able to grow at the expense of rivals and had the constant threat from the *emishi* to keep them in trim.

These developments are illustrated by the revolt of Taira Masakado in AD 935. Masakado, as his name implies, came from a branch of the Taira clan, which was to achieve great power in the following century. His rebellion, which went as far as Masakado proclaiming himself as a rival Emperor, produced a serious challenge both to the ruling house and to the other law-abiding members of the Taira family. It was in fact his own clan which was instrumental in bringing about his death in AD 940. *Konjaku Monogatari*, the twelfth-century chronicle which covers the rebellion, includes in its narrative some important guidelines as to how the idea of an élite samurai class was emerging and what its values were. One theme that comes over is the move towards a certain exclusivity of the samurai class, membership of which is a privilege so universally accepted that it is felt necessary to make some comment when this factor is absent. One example is the comment on a particular samurai that 'although he did not belong to a

PLATE 2　*A provincial samurai, in a poor quality armour, ca 1160*

The samurai who fought for the Minamoto cause in the early campaigns of the Gempei War were regarded as rough and vulgar characters by the more sophisticated Taira clan. This plate, which is based on a section of the *Heiji Monogatari Emaki* in the Museum of Fine Arts, Boston, Massachussetts, is an attempt to realise such a rough, unshaven warrior. His heavy helmet (copied from an extant specimen in the Oyamazumi Shrine Museum, Omishima, Hiroshima Prefecture) with its wide *fukigayeshi* (turnbacks) and *shikoro* (neckguard) has a minimum of decoration, the finish of the metal bowl being a natural coating of rust. His suit of armour is the simple *do-maru*, lacking the leather breastplate of his betters, but he enjoys a better protection than a common footsoldier by wearing two large *sode* or shoulder-plates. His pole-arm is a very plain *naginata*, which he is carefully sheathing after use. Note that, even though his main weapon is not the bow, he wears no armour on his right sleeve, in true samurai tradition. His armour is laced with leather thongs.

A warrior from the period between the fifth and seventh centuries AD wearing a *tanko*, the solid plate form of body-armour that preceded the adoption of lamellar styles. This statue is in the Gifu Historical Museum.

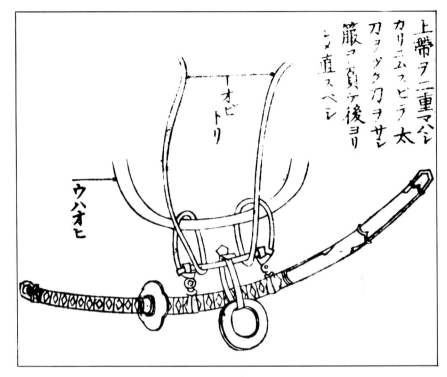

One way recommended by the *Gunyoki* for wearing the slung sword, the *tachi*, and the reel holding a spare bowstring. The cords of the sword are looped around a belt, the *uwa-obi*, thus giving additional support.

warrior house, he was courageous and accomplished in the Way of Bow and Arrow'. This latter phrase, *kyusen no michi*, otherwise rendered as *kyuba no michi*, 'The Way of Horse and Bow', is the obvious precursor of the much later *bushido*, 'The Way of the Warrior', and implies the existence of certain standards of conduct and accomplishment which are by rights the prerogative of an élite, though not, as yet, the élite's exclusive possession. A further example is found in the *Shoyuki*, the diary of the venerable old Fujiwara Sanesuke (957–1046). Here Sanesuke refers disparagingly to a distant relative called Fujiwara Norimoto, who killed one of his own vassals. 'Norimoto enjoys the martial arts', writes Sanesuke, 'but people do not approve. He is not of warrior blood.'

The struggle for land is a fundamental theme throughout samurai history. Sometimes it was gained by outright warfare, but territory could often be acquired by being granted a high office of state with lands attached, and the conflicts for such appointments could be as bitter as direct campaigns for the acquisition of territory. Taira Masakado's revolt occurred because he was refused the important office of *kebiishi*, an appointment concerned with the arrest and punishment of criminals. An order given by the *kebiishi* carried with it the full weight of Imperial authority and many warrior houses gained their early reputations by delivering the heads of criminals to Kyoto and collecting rewards such as provincial governorships. To become a provincial governor made a samurai into a petty prince, taking his considerable share of the produce of the lands entrusted to his care. *Kebiishi* was thus a coveted position.

17

Provincial governors were not always benevolent. One notorious example is Taira Korehira, son of the vanquisher of Masakado, who at various times was granted governorships of the provinces of Ise, Mutsu, Dewa, Izu, Shimotsuke, Sado, Kozuke and Hitachi. Not that he governed any of them very well. His successor in Hitachi complained that the people were starving and Korehira eventually ended his disappointing career by making open war against his kinsman Muneyori. For this he was apprehended and was exiled to the island of Awaji in the Inland Sea.

The Classical Samurai

The most important series of events in the history of the samurai was the process by which these élite, land-owning fighters transformed their condition from being the servants of Emperors and quellers of rebels and barbarians to being the *de facto* government of Japan, reducing the Emperor to a mere figurehead under their military dictatorship. This revolution happened during the latter part of the twelfth century AD, and is centred around a civil war between two clans, the Minamoto and the Taira, called the Gempei War.

Both the Minamoto and the Taira descended from branches of the Imperial family. Both had ancestors whose valiant exploits had set the standard against which their samurai measured their own accomplishments, and both were enormously ambitious. Each clan held numerous rice-lands and provided a focus for the adherents who served them as farmers and samurai and occasionally married into the family. The strength of the Taira was concentrated in the West of Japan. Their 'family temple' was the beautiful Itsukushima Shrine built out onto the sea of the island of Miyajima in the Inland Sea. They had great influence at Court, bought by years of service to succeeding Emperors.

PLATE 3 *A warrior monk from Mount Hiei, ca 1170*

A prominent feature of the warfare of eleventh-and twelfth-century Japan was the use of armies of *sohei*, or warrior monks, by the great Buddhist foundations of Kyoto and Nara. The *sohei* shown here wears a costume typical of these fierce fighters. The long white monk's robe, which is gathered at the ankles, is augmented by a simple footsoldier's *do-maru* armour, consisting of a tube-like corselet of lacquered leather or iron plates laced together with leather or cord thongs.

It has seven *kusazuri*, or skirt pieces. On top is worn a thin black, gauze-like outer robe, and the sword hangs outside it, through the deep slashes at the waist. The traditional headgear was either a knotted towel around the shaven pate, or the elaborate headcowl shown in this illustration, which reached almost to nose level and was tied behind the head. He carries the traditional weapon of the warrior monks – the *naginata* – and is depicted standing outside one of the hundreds of

shrines on Mount Hiei, to the North-West of Kyoto. The main foundation of Mount Hiei, the Enryaku-ji, was a Buddhist temple, but the mountain was also sacred to a Shinto deity, Sanno, the Mountain King, hence the *torii* gateway behind him.

The picture is based on several sources, notably the scrolls *Tengu Zoshi emaki* (Tokyo National Museum) and *Kasuga Gongen Reikenki* (Imperial Household Collection).

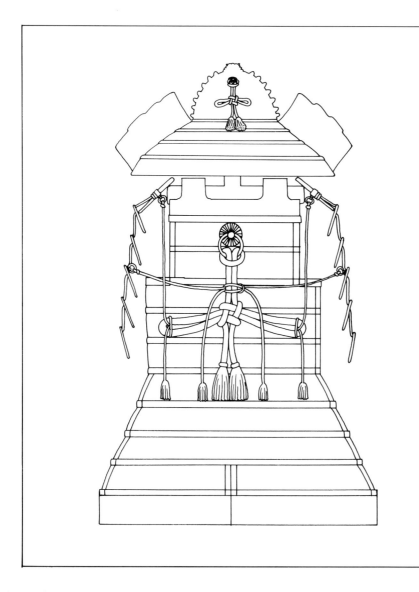

The *agemaki* bow
The decorative *agemaki* bow was the means whereby the various parts of a *yoroi* armour were held together at the rear. It was suspended from a ring on the upper plate of the back, and the various cords, shown in the first drawing, connected it to the *sode* (shoulder-plates), thereby holding them back to allow the arms free movement. The second and third drawings show how the *agemaki* was formed from one long cord.

The Minamoto's power lay in the less-civilised East where there were still *emishi* to fight. Their family temple was the striking Tsurugaoka Hachiman Shrine in Kamakura, dedicated to Hachiman, the Shinto God of War. These 'Eastern Warriors' were spoken of disparagingly by the more sophisticated West and, in the early days of the clans' struggle, the differences were probably quite marked. The troops of Minamoto Yoshinaka (1154–1184), for example, were regarded as rough mountain men, whose appearance and manners alone alarmed the people of the capital and did much to erode his support. Yoshinaka's own uncouth and ambitious presence eventually led to his death at the hands of his cousin Yoritomo.

By contrast the Taira samurai are often portrayed as accomplished poets and refined courtiers. Nor was this far from the truth, for by the 1170s the

The 'Home Provinces' of Japan. Until modern times this central area of Japan between Kyoto and Osaka, bordered to the north-east by Lake Biwa, and to the south by the mountains of the Kii peninsula, was the pivot around which much of Japanese history revolved.

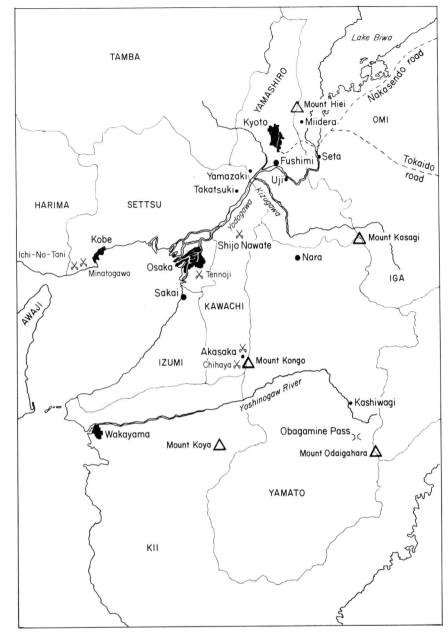

Taira had risen to a point of political pre-eminence by the straightforward process of marrying their daughters to Imperial princes. There was nothing particularly revolutionary about this – the Fujiwara clan had been doing it for centuries, and the Taira was merely the first other family to try the same game. It meant, however, that the Taira, in the person of the clan head, Taira Kiyomori, an astute politician, had gained political power by using and manipulating existing political institutions which they served as loyal samurai. It was the Minamoto who were to provide the samurai revolution.

21

The early samurai battles of the Gempei War are notable for the presence of a third force – contingents of warrior monks, or *sohei*. Several of the great monasteries of Kyoto and Nara maintained armies for defence in the lawless times, and would readily use them against rival temples or samurai armies. The fiercest coterie of warrior monks belonged to the Enryaku-ji, the main temple on Mount Hiei, which lies to the North-East of Kyoto, an area regarded as the abode of several very powerful *kami*, the Shinto word for a spiritual divinity. Mount Hiei also provided a natural fortress, and a standing army of several thousand monks, and we will see regular references to support being sought from the warrior monks of Mount Hiei as late as the sixteenth century. They were formidable warriors, though unreliable as allies, for they always put the interests of their temples first. In their early disputes the fear of the *kami* they represented was often enough to frighten the Imperial Court into granting their demands. They would march on Kyoto carrying the sacred *mikoshi*, or portable shrine, in which the *kami* was supposed to dwell. If the Imperial Court would not grant their wishes, which were usually concerned with land rights or prestige, the *mikoshi* would be left in the city street until a different decision was reached. Few samurai had such fear of the monks, but they would earn great approbation for standing up to them.

The war between the Taira and the Minamoto was a struggle for supremacy into which all social classes were drawn. The first Taira/Minamoto struggle in which the monks fought was the First Battle of Uji in 1180. The veteran warrior, Minamoto Yorimasa, raised the flag of rebellion against the Taira while he was still based in Kyoto – a very risky operation. His monkish support came from the temple of Onjo-ji, or Miidera, which lies at the foot of Mount Hiei and had a long history of stubborn independence from the Enryaku-ji on the summit. When Yorimasa's plot

PLATE 4   *A general being dressed by a page in a fine* yoroi, *ca 1180*

This plate provides a direct comparison between the military costume of the highest and lowest ranking samurai of the Gempei War Period. The *taisho* (general) is completely armed except for his helmet. Note that instead of the hair being gathered into a pigtail it has been let down. The stiff *eboshi* cap will be removed before the helmet is placed on to the head. This may indicate that the helmet has a separate lining. The *yoroi* armour is little different from that shown in Plate 1, except that it is more richly ornamented with gilt fittings, as befits the wearer, and is based on an extant specimen in the Oyamazumi Shrine Museum, Omishima (Hiroshima Prefecture). His *yoroi-hitatare*, or armour robe, is richly embroidered and ornamented with pom-poms. His attendant is tying the general's quiver securely round his waist in such a position that arrows may be easily withdrawn with the right hand. The arrows are held in place in the basket-like quiver by twisted cords that are wound round the quiver's back. As the general is of such exalted rank he has been depicted wearing footwear while indoors! The interior design is based on the contemporary Genji Monogatari Scroll.

The attendant's costume, which appears to change little for four centuries, is based on the simple *do-maru* we noted on the warrior monk. His black *eboshi* cap, tied with cords, is of similar design to the general's. When going into battle it would be augmented by the face-mask seen in Plate 5. His small shoulder-protectors are of padded cloth, possibly strengthened within by metal or leather plates. As he is not an archer he wears two *kote* (armour sleeves) which are simple cloth bags with metal plates sewn on at strategic places.

was discovered he and his warrior monks decided to retreat South, across the Uji River, to join forces with the warrior monks of the Kofuku-ji at Nara. The Uji River, which flows out of Lake Biwa to join the Yodo River, entering the sea near Osaka, has always been a natural moat to Kyoto, and the two bridges at Seta and Uji were strategic prizes for any army wishing to take the capital or, as in Yorimasa's case, safeguard his flight from it. The Taira forces followed in pursuit, so the Minamoto tore up the planking of the Uji bridge and prepared to make a stand until the Nara monks could join them. After much fierce fighting, and gallant acts of swordsmanship while balanced on the beams of the broken bridge, the Taira samurai succeeded in crossing the river and Yorimasa, completely surrounded, committed suicide.

The act of suicide when faced with certain defeat is a well-known tradition concerned with samurai warfare. Suicide could also be taken as an alternative to execution, as a means of apologising for a wrong deed while saving one's honour and, more rarely, as a highly dramatic act of protest. Yet suicide was never an automatic act. We frequently hear of samurai fleeing, withdrawing and, occasionally, surrendering, though the latter is very often followed by the suicide of the captive. As we shall see in the following pages the omission of suicide is sometimes more surprising than its commission.

Minamoto Yoshitsune

A large part of the accounts of the Gempei War is taken up by descriptions of the long campaigns of Minamoto Yoshitsune, the Minamoto's ablest general, and one of the most famous samurai who ever existed. He is best known for his battles against the Taira, but he began his career by defeating his cousin, the rough man from the mountains, Minamoto Yoshinaka.

Yoshinaka had in fact served the Minamoto cause well, by defeating the Taira at the Battle of Tonamiyama (or Kurikara) in 1182, where he had succeeded in forcing the Taira army into a dead-end valley by stampeding a herd of cattle, enraged by tying lighted torches to their horns. As a result he succeeded in being the first of the Minamoto to enter the capital in triumph, where his men behaved very badly. It was probably Yoshinaka's very success that set his cousins against him, rather than any genuine concern for the inhabitants whom his men had abused. Yoshitsune was sent to the West to chastise him and met Yoshinaka's force at the Uji River. Unlike Yorimasa in 1180, however, who was fighting off an attack from the capital, Yoshinaka attempted to use it in reverse. But once again a successful crossing was made and Yoshinaka withdrew with a handful of followers, until his horse crashed through the ice of a frozen paddy field. As Yoshinaka turned in the saddle an arrow hit him in the face. Two samurai ran up and struck off his head.

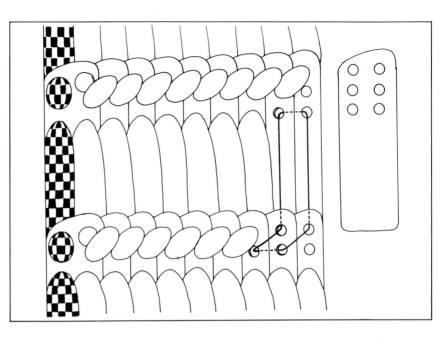

Kebiki-odoshi lacing – detail
This shows the way in which the cords of a _kebiki-odoshi_ (laced armour) interrelated. The outer line of cords was often of a multicoloured weave, known as 'woodpecker braid'.

With Yoshinaka's personal ambitions out of the way the main branch of the Minamoto could concentrate on the defeat of the Taira, who had possession of the child Emperor, grandson of Taira Kiyomori. To be seen to be acting in the name of the Emperor, even if he was virtually a hostage, was an important guarantee of support. The other great strength of the Taira was their command of the sea. They had their own fleet and a network of bases along the Inland Sea. On three occasions they withstood attacks from Yoshitsune while based either on the sea or very near to it. The first was the Battle of Ichi-no-tani in 1184. Ichi-no-tani was a stockade-type fortress on the shore of the Inland Sea near to the present-day city of Kobe. It was defended on two sides by palisades, while the third was open to the sea where the escape craft lay, and the rear was defended by steep cliffs. Yoshitsune's attack shows his imagination and daring. While two groups of samurai attacked from the sides, he led a picked band of men down a precipitous path at the rear and took the Taira completely by surprise. There was no wild panic for the boats – samurai honour would not have permitted that. Instead a number of individual combats took place on the shore, several of which, such as the death of the young Taira samurai, Atsumori, quickly entered the pantheon of samurai heroics as being perfect examples of the death of the brave, lone warrior – an image cherished throughout samurai history. But the bulk of the Taira escaped, taking with them the child-Emperor Antoku, whose capture was their main aim.

A few months later Yoshitsune pursued them to Yashima on the island of Shikoku. Here the battle was fought in the shallows which divided the then island of Yashima from Shikoku. It was fiercely contested, but one celebrated incident which occurred during the fighting shows that the tradition of the samurai as an élite mounted archer was still as strong as

25

ever. During a lull in the fighting the Taira had tied a fan to the mast of one of their ships and challenged the Minamoto to shoot it down, hoping thereby to encourage them to waste their ammunition. The challenge was accepted by Nasu Munetaka, a young samurai retainer of the Minamoto, who took careful aim as the fan fluttered in the breeze and shattered it with his first shot, which greatly improved the Minamoto morale.

The Battle of Yashima was as indecisive as Ichi-no-tani had been, as the child Emperor was once again spirited away by sea. But it served to illustrate that the Minamoto were determined to pursue the Taira wherever they led. The final reckoning came in April 1185, when both armies met in a sea battle at Dan-no-Ura in the Straits of Shimonoseki, the narrow gap of water that divides Honshu from Kyushu. The fighting was long and hard, and a sea battle only in the sense of two armies using ships as fighting platforms for archers and swordsmen, for there is very little of naval manoeuvring to be discerned. Dan-no-Ura ended with the utter defeat of the Taira, and one of the largest mass suicides in samurai history as the Taira reeled from an overwhelming attack. The child-Emperor Antoku was drowned and the replica Sacred Sword, one of the three items that comprise the Japanese Imperial Regalia, was lost forever. So terrible was the eclipse of the Taira clan at Dan-no-Ura that many legends grew up concerning ghosts, seas of blood, and crabs with the spirits of samurai within them. It is still regarded as one of the most decisive battles in Japanese history.

Minamoto Yoshitsune, however, was not the clan member who benefited from the defeat of its rivals. His elder brother Yoritomo was head of the clan, and it was Yoritomo who was to take over where the Taira had left off, and found a dynasty to rule the country in the name of the Emperor. Where Yoritomo's achievement differed from that of the Taira, however, was that instead of making use of existing institutions of Imperial government, and marrying daughters into the family, Yoritomo founded a new system of hereditary military government under a dictator known as the *shogun*, a word that is nowadays as familiar as *samurai*. In 1192 Minamoto Yoritomo became the first Minamoto Shogun, ruling by means of a Shogunal government or *bakufu*. The Minamoto triumph was complete, as was the total ascendancy of the samurai military élite.

PLATE 5   *A footsoldier in a* do-maru, *ca 1184*

This common footsoldier is taken directly from an illustration in the scroll *Kasuga Gongen Reikenki*. He is on guard duty outside a samurai headquarters in Kyoto. His costume is very similar to that of the footsoldiers in Plates 4 and 6 except that he wears a metal face-protector that covers the forehead and cheeks, and provides some defence against a sword slash. His shoulder-protectors are covered by a dyed leather similar to that used for the 'breastplate' of a samurai's armour. Details of the scenery are taken from the Heiji Monogatari Scroll.

2

Kamakura Period

The establishment of Minamoto Yoritomo's Shogunate, or *bakufu*, marks the beginning of the 'Kamakura Period' in Japanese history, from 1192 until 1333, as the city of Kamakura was the seat of the Shogun and thus the administrative capital of Japan.

The Fall of the Minamoto

The Kamakura *bakufu* was never all-powerful, in spite of the dramatic way it had been formed, and had to face a continued resistance to the Shogunal power from the Imperial family. As we shall see, it was to be the power of an Emperor that finally brought about its downfall. There is one other remarkable feature about the Kamakura Period: that the Minamoto, the family whose triumph seems so complete in 1192, should so soon be vanquished as thoroughly as they had destroyed the Taira.

In view of the tremendous achievement of Yoritomo in raising his family to the highest position in the land, it is strange that their dynasty should turn out to be so short-lived. Apart from the earlier destruction of Yoshinaka, the first feuding within the family was Yoritomo's personal rivalry with his brothers Yoshitsune and Noriyori, whose military skills had helped him gain the position of Shogun. Both were driven from office and pursued to death. Perhaps fittingly Yoritomo himself enjoyed only 7 years as Shogun, dying in 1199, at the age of 52, when he was thrown from a horse while returning in state from a public ceremony. His death was accidental, untimely, and threw the whole *bakufu* into confusion. His 18-year-old son Yoriie immediately succeeded to his late father's civil offices, but there was a long delay in having him appointed Shogun. Many Kamakura officials had expressed genuine concern about the young man's ability to govern, but in fact the whole of the government had been so thoroughly shaken by Yoritomo's unexpected death that it was left to his widow, Masa-ko, to form a provisional government together with her father Hojo Tokimasa.

Masa-ko comes over as a very strong-willed woman. She had entered the religious life on her husband's death, as was the custom of the times, but her vows do not seem to have diminished her political skills and ambi-

One of the most historic places associated with the samurai is the Tsurugaoka Hachiman Shrine at Kamakura. It is always thronged with visitors. It is dedicated to Hachiman, the God of War, and was particularly honoured by the Minamoto clan, although this picture illustrates two tragic aspects of the history of that great samurai family. In the foreground is the dancing platform where Shizuka Gozen, the lover of the fugitive Minamoto Yoshitsune, was forced to dance for Yoshitsune's brother, Yoritomo, the first Shogun of Japan. Shizuka defiantly sang a song in praise of Yoshitsune, an act which enraged the dictator, and when she gave birth to a male child he had the baby murdered. To the left is a very large, and very old gingko tree, which may well be the actual one behind which lurked the assassin of the third and last Minamoto Shogun, Sanetomo, one snowy day in 1219.

tions, for she is referred to as *ama shogun*, the 'Nun Shogun'. Her provisional government, however, was not a success in bringing about the unity the country required and, when Yoriie was eventually proclaimed Shogun in 1202, little had been done to assist the headstrong young man in his rule of the warriors. Then Yoriie became gravely ill and within a year had been forced to retire, sick and humiliated, from the post of Shogun. He withdrew totally from public life and entered a monastery, only to be assassinated in 1204, probably at the instigation of his grandfather, Hojo Tokimasa.

Yoriie had a son, but the Hojo influence in the *bakufu* was so strong that his succession was passed over in favour of Yoriie's younger brother Sanetomo, who was then only 12 years old. Sanetomo became the third and last Minamoto Shogun and, as he was a minor, a Regent was necessary, a role Hojo Tokimasa was ready to fulfil. Tokimasa therefore became the first of a long line of *shikken*, the Hojo Regents, who ruled behind a nominal Shogun for a century and a half.

But even with the power of the Minamoto so dramatically curtailed, Sanetomo was doomed to enjoy for a very short time the honours of office. In the New Year of 1219 Sanetomo proceeded to the Tsurugaoka Hachiman Shrine in Kamakura to give thanks to Hachiman, the patron deity of the Minamoto, for the favours which his clan had received. As he was walking down the snow-covered steps of the shrine, a figure jumped out from behind a gingko tree and stabbed him to death. He was 26 years old. Legend has embellished the facts of his murder, which was as much a tragedy for Japanese culture as it was for the family of Minamoto.

Sanetomo was a noted poet, and legend tells of how he was warned of the threat to his life, but declined his attendant's suggestion that he should wear armour under his robe. Instead he wrote a farewell poem, and left a lock of his hair behind as a memento.

His nephew Kugyo, whose succession had been ignored, was the natural suspect for instigating the murder plot, and the deed provided the perfect excuse for having him, the last in the Minamoto line, executed. This was the final act of the blood-letting that makes the clan of Minamoto sound like the subjects of Greek tragedy. For the next 100 years power was kept by the 'Nun Shogun's' family, the Hojo, who had so thoroughly eclipsed them.

The Jokyu War

The establishment of the Shogunate may have weakened the Imperial power, but little could negate the magic in the name of the divine Emperor, and we see throughout samurai history successive Emperors of Japan, sometimes manipulated and reduced to ceremony, sometimes defiant and proud, but always exerting the charisma that comes from unquestioned legitimacy. The fall of the Minamoto showed the comparatively weak base of any alternative ruler.

The great problem which faced the rule of the Hojo *shikken* was to find a succession of suitable candidates for Shogun, in whose names they could rule as Regent, so it was almost inevitable that the Imperial family should

PLATE 6 *Hojo Yasutoki, in 'half-armour', inspects heads after the Jokyu Rebellion, 1221*

From ancient times the surest proof that a samurai had performed the task with which he had been entrusted was for him to return to his master bearing the severed head of the enemy. Elaborate rituals grew up over how heads were presented, prepared and examined. The business of preparing severed heads was traditionally done by the women of the clan, and there exist accounts of how the heads were washed, drained of blood and mounted on a spiked wooden board. The hair would be neatly combed from the mess which battle would have caused and tied with white paper into the traditional samurai pigtail. The heads would be anointed with perfume by waving an incense burner under them, and cosmetics applied to recreate the colours they would have possessed in life. The final touch was provided by tying a slip of paper to each pigtail, giving the name of the dead samurai, the name of the samurai whose 'trophy' the head had become, and any other relevant details. In the case of a shaven-headed monk the absence of a pigtail meant that a hole had to be made in the ear-lobe to take the identifying document!

Head-viewing ceremonies could be very elaborate, as they were an important part of public relations. By head-viewing, a victorious general was given the opportunity of commenting upon an ally's achievements and making a forcible point to newly subordinate clans of the folly of opposing such a glorious band of samurai.

This plate is a reconstruction of the head-viewing ceremony that must have taken place following the collapse of ex-Emperor Go-Toba's Jokyu Rebellion of 1221. The victorious general, Hojo Yasutoki, sits on a tiger-skin rug on a camp stool in 'undress armour', which shows what was worn under the main body-armour of the *yoroi*. The extent of the sleeve bag on the left arm is clearly seen, and also how the separate portion of the *yoroi* fitted under the right arm. His *eboshi* is a courtier style, which is much larger than that normally worn under a helmet. The footsoldiers wear simple body-armours.

The label on the monk's head reads 'The head of a brave warrior monk: Hojo Yasutoki'. The other labels credit their trophies to Yasutoki's uncle, Hojo Tokifusa, who also took part in the downfall of Go-Toba's rebellion.

try to take advantage of this potential weakness whenever possible, and the early thirteenth century provided such a challenge in the person of the ex-Emperor Go-Toba. The Emperor Go-Toba had succeeded to the throne in 1184, at the age of 4, and soon learned the lesson of all Emperors that true power only came about following abdication, when they could rule behind the scenes, freed from the long round of religious ritual, which, as living god, the Emperor was required to perform. He was still too young to become such a Retired, or 'Cloistered' Emperor when Go-Shirakawa died in 1192, and 1192 was also the year when Yoritomo achieved the Shogunate, reducing all Imperial power to a very low ebb. He eventually managed to abdicate in 1198, and tested his new powers by appointing his infant son, Tsuchimikado, to the vacant throne without asking permission from Kamakura. Yoritomo was much annoyed, but before he could assert his Shogunal authority he had suffered the fatal accident which was eventually to destroy the Minamoto clan. Go-Toba played a careful game through the troubled years of Yoriie and Sanetomo and was, in fact, on very good terms with the latter, as he shared his love for poetry, but when Sanetomo was murdered Go-Toba realised that the Hojo's need for a puppet successor to the Shogunate might provide an opportunity for the throne to assert itself more strongly than it had for half a century.

The first suggestion the Regent Hojo Yoshitoki made was that one of Go-Toba's own sons should become Shogun. Go-Toba refused the apparent honour, as he saw the potential danger that could arise if there was a succession dispute when an Imperial prince was Shogun. He then turned down a candidate from the Fujiwara family and, in fact, managed to frustrate for several years every one of the Hojo's attempts to have a Shogun appointed. In the meantime he openly courted the favour of any rival samurai families who might one day join him in armed struggle against the Shogunate for the restoration of Imperial power. There were a number of clans in the Western half of the country who could be persuaded to support him. Some were the remnants of the once mighty Taira, others mere opportunists who had suffered from the Minamoto or Hojo ascendancy. But they were only one factor in Go-Toba's scheme. The other involved seeking support from that most dangerous and unreliable of weapons: the warrior monks.

The armed clergy had been very peaceful during Yoritomo's lifetime. The first Shogun had been generous with his gifts towards rebuilding temples

PLATE 7 *A samurai commander awaits the Mongol Invasion in 1274*

His armour has altered to no appreciable degree since the time of the Gempei War, evidence that, until the coming of the Mongols, there was little to challenge any samurai assumptions about the nature of warfare. He is seated on an armour box, into which his *yoroi* would be packed for careful storage.

damaged during the Gempei War, but in common with every other faction in the land they had become rebellious when the Shogunate was seen to be weakening. In 1219 the old rivalry between the Enryaku-ji and Miidera once more flared into life, and the Kofuku-ji of Nara also began to rediscover its warlike traditions. A land dispute provided the excuse for the Mount Hiei monks to try their mettle against Go-Toba, and in the manner which had been so successful with his predecessors they descended on Kyoto to lay their grievances before the throne with threats and riot. But times had changed. Instead of being cowed by the threats of divine vengeance Go-Toba scattered their incursion by a well-timed assault from the palace samurai. However, in further contrast, he followed up this lesson not with a revenge attack on the Enryaku-ji, but with a carefully worded call to arms against the Shogun on the Emperor's behalf, asking them to unite against the warriors from the East who had shown so little respect for the monks' militant and religious tradition.

Go-Toba began an open revolt against the *bakufu* on 6 June 1221, when by solemn decree the Regent Hojo Yoshitoki was declared to be an outlaw. Three days later a further statement was made decreeing the whole of the Eastern half of the country to be in a state of rebellion. Both announcements were designed to catch Kamakura unawares, but a relay of fast messengers had managed to warn Yoshitoki of the former proclamation by the day the latter was issued, and he immediately took steps to assure himself of the loyalty of neighbouring samurai. His support was solid, and plans were quickly made.

Their first consideration was one of defence, of closing the passes of Ashigara and Hakone, in the Mount Fuji area, to prevent any advance on Kamakura by the Tokaido Road. But bolder spirits argued that attack would be the better response to the Imperial forces, so a plan was drawn up involving a march on Kyoto by means of the three practical routes: the Tokaido along the Sea Coast, the Nakasendo through the central mountains, and a wide sweep off the Nakasendo going round Lake Biwa to approach Kyoto from the north. This third column met with the most resistance. There were still several clans in the Hokurikudo region who had not accepted Kamakura rule, and the Hojo forces were held for a while at Tonamiyama, the site of Yoshinaka's fierce battle in the Gempei War, but this fighting in Echizen Province proved to be the only serious resistance Kamakura faced and, by the time the Hokurikudo column had fought its way down from the mountains, the capital was already in *bakufu* hands. The Imperial troops were largely inexperienced and had little will to fight the warriors from the East, whose fathers' reputations had preceded their advance Westwards. Many of the defenders fled from their positions in Mino and Omi Provinces, putting their trust in the natural moat of the Uji River, so for the third time in half a century the two bridges of Uji and Seta echoed to the din of war. But this time there were no warrior monks to stride nimbly with their *naginata* across the broken planking, for in spite of all Go-Toba's pleas the *sohei* of the Enryaku-ji remained on Mount Hiei,

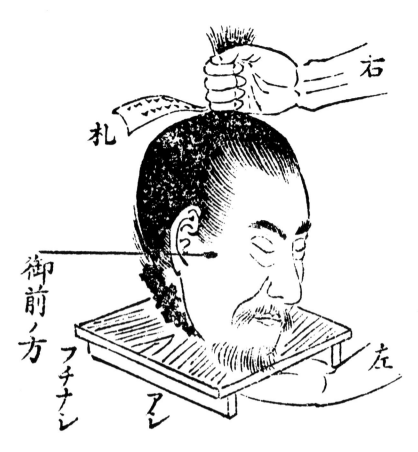

This illustration from the *Gunyoki* is one of several recommended ways of displaying a severed head. Note the carefully delineated positions of the hands, the identification label, and the spiked wooden board.

and it was an almost totally secular force that attempted to hold the line on 5 July. The fighting of this, the Third Battle of Uji, lasted all through a hot summer's day, but by nightfall Hojo Yasutoki's men had taken Seta, in spite of heavy losses, and the road to Kyoto was open.

Hojo Yasutoki (who was Yoshitoki's eldest son) made a grand entrance on the following day, 6 July, his scouts having prepared the city for his arrival. Unfortunately many of the retreating troops, and some of the Hojo's advance guard, had burned and looted as they went, and the Imperial capital presented a sorry spectacle when the *bakufu* army received the surrender of Go-Toba.

Thus ended the brief Jokyu Rebellion, so called from the era name of Jokyu (1219–1221). The *bakufu's* triumph was due largely to its boldness in advancing. Had their original consideration of a defensive strategy been put into effect it is quite likely that Go-Toba's support would have continued to grow to an extent dangerous to the Shogunate. In the event Go-Toba was exiled and the *bakufu* confiscated the largest area of defeated enemies' lands since the fall of the Taira. The Minamoto may have passed away, but even without the figurehead of a Shogun to lead them, the Hojo *shikken* proved that the institution of warrior government which Yoritomo had established was sufficiently sound to withstand even a challenge from an ex-Emperor. It was to be 50 years before any other military threat arose and, when it came, it was very different from anything the samurai had faced before.

The Mongol Invasions

The attempts to invade Japan made in the thirteenth century by the Mongol Emperor of China, Kublai Khan, are unique events in Japanese history. The ferocity with which the attacks were launched, the strength and bravery of the resistance, and the final, sudden and spectacular end of the Mongol fleet by a typhoon fill some of the noblest pages in the history of the samurai.

Kublai Khan, it must be admitted, had reasons for invading Japan other than mere personal ambition. The pressing demands of various civil wars had caused *bakufu* officials in Kyushu responsible for maintaining law and order to turn a blind eye towards a frequent abuse of their authority — overseas piracy. The coastal areas of China and Korea were frequently ravaged by Japanese pirates and Kublai Khan's first letter to the Japanese government was simply a request that such activities be curtailed. It was only when he received no reply to this demand that his theme became one of demanding tribute from the Japanese people. It was fortunate for Japan that it faced the challenge under the Hojo Regent Tokimune, the seventh of the *shikken* and a capable and resourceful samurai. It was also free from civil strife so it was possible to make a positive response to the threat.

PLATE 8   *Kusunoki Masashige defends Chihaya castle, 1333*

The mid-fourteenth century is dominated by the epic struggle of the War Between the Courts. This plate depicts the greatest hero of that war, the loyal samurai, Kusunoki Masashige (1294–1336). He is shown conducting operations in the forests around Mount Kongo, where he established his bases of Akasaka and Chihaya, and defied the Kamakura *bakufu*. His defence of Chihaya, in particular, is regarded as one of the three classic sieges of samurai history when defenders withstood enormous odds and never capitulated.

Kusunoki Masashige is wearing what is basically a *yoroi* armour, but with several developments. First, the *yoroi* has lost something of its stiff, box-like appearance and fits the body more closely, like a footsoldier's *haramaki*. It still has the

tsurubashiri, the leather 'breastplate', and Masashige's is very beautifully decorated. An *agemaki* bow would connect all the pieces from the rear.

The helmet's *shikoro* is now much flatter, which would allow the wearer to turn his head more easily, while its greater sweep still allows good protection. His helmet bowl is neater. The conical rivets have disappeared, and it is ornamented by a particularly fine set of *kuwagata*.

It is in his leg protection that we notice the greatest difference. The *suneate* are much heavier and extend up higher to surround the knee. The thighs are now protected by an early form of *haidate*, or thigh-guards, which are of exactly similar construction to the plates of the body-armour, and fasten behind the leg. Bearskin boots have given way to the more practical *waraji*, straw

sandals, and *tabi*, the traditional Japanese sock with a divided toe.

The long, red-lacquered bow is well represented here, for even though horsemanship is irrelevant in the wooded mountains, the samurai is still an archer. Note the waterproof quiver, and the arrow being brought to the bow from the righthand side, in the Japanese style of archery.

The figure is based on the modern statue of Kusunoki Masashige at the Kanshin-ji near Chihaya, where Masashige's head is buried, and painted scrolls kept at the Nampi-an Kannon-ji, also near Chihaya. Details of his body-armour are taken from a *yoroi* of the period preserved in the Kasuga Shrine at Nara which is supposed to have been owned by Masashige. Details of accessories and leg-armour are taken from a sketch by Sasama.

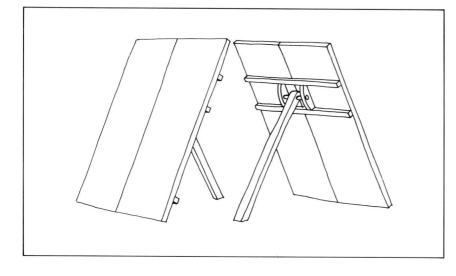

The wooden shield
This type of wooden shield was used throughout the samurai period. It was planted in the ground, and provided protection for missile troops. Contemporary illustrations often depict them with *mon* painted on the front.

The first attack came in 1274. The Khan swelled his army with sub-servient Koreans and packed them into several hundred ships. They first attacked Tsushima, the island mid-way between Japan and Korea, where the garrison of 200 men under So Sukekuni, grandson of Taira Tomomori, who was drowned at Dan-no-Ura, fought bravely until they were overwhelmed. The next island, Ikishima, suffered a similar fate. Their attempt on the Japanese mainland (in fact the large Southern island of Kyushu) took place near the present-day city of Hakata. The Japanese resistance was fierce, in spite of several surprises that the Mongols were able to inflict on the defenders, for their military traditions were totally different from the samurai. The Japanese were used to a style of warfare that laid great emphasis on individual combat, while the Mongols controlled, by drum and gong, huge bodies of troops packed together in phalanxes, and fired arrows in huge random showers. There were no noble opponents to challenge to individual combat, just an anonymous alien horde of Mongols, Chinese and Koreans. Their enemies also had some form of fire-bomb, flung by catapult, which is illustrated in a painted scroll of the period. The samurai very quickly adapted to all these new threats and their fighting skills forced the Mongols into a tactical withdrawal. A storm caught the fleet as it left, causing much damage, and the first invasion came to a end.

The Mongols returned in 1281 with a much bigger armada. By this time coastal defences had been strengthened, including the building of a long stone wall, and the Japanese also managed to harass the fleet as it approached the coast. They sailed out in little ships and mounted daring hit-and-run raids under the cover of darkness. On one occasion thirty samurai swam out to a ship, cut off the heads of the crew, and swam back. Apart from the direct damage the raids were able to inflict, these raids also had the considerable benefit of forcing the Mongol fleet to remain for long periods lying safely offshore in the stifling heat of summer. As the days wore on, the typhoon season approached and, on 15 August 1281, the Japanese prayers were answered when a fierce storm, the *kami-kaze,* blew up. It surpassed in intensity the storm that had damaged the fleet in 1274 and smashed the Mongol fleet so totally that they never returned.

Few episodes in Japanese history are as proudly recalled as the defeat of the Mongols. To the defeat of the Mongols we owe the phrase *kami-kaze* (divine wind), an expression which came to have such a different meaning in 1945, when it linked the threat of an American invasion with the failed attempts of 1274 and 1281, inspiring a new generation to resist an assault on the homeland. It has in it all the finest elements of Japanese tradition. There are noble samurai, united against a common enemy, and fired by a common spirit which later manifests itself in the cataclysm of the holy typhoon. For once in their history the samurai are not fighting each other, but become Japanese before anything else.

The War of Emperor Go-Daigo

The defeat of the Mongols saw the samurai united as never before, yet within two generations they were to be divided on the most fundamental issue of their tradition: that of the legitimacy of their divine Emperor. The attempts of a young Emperor, Go-Daigo, to rule, rather than merely to reign, caused a schism in the Imperial House, and a long civil war.

The destruction of the Mongol fleet may have been a military victory for the *bakufu,* but one long-term result was to produce severe economic strain on the government. No one could be sure that the Mongols would not return, so they faced the need to be prepared against foreign invasion for half a century. Rewards also had to be paid to samurai who had fought in the wars, and there were no freshly conquered lands to redistribute, as would have been the case in a civil war. Numerous claims were made. One samurai even had a long narrative scroll painted depicting his exploits as an aid to his demands. Temples and shrines too, mindful of the miraculous intervention of the *kami-kaze,* put in claims for reward as a mark of appreciation of their spiritual efforts. Hojo Tokimune, whose leadership had proved such an inspiration to the samurai, died in 1284, and his successors failed completely to inherit his abilities and drive. As at the time of Jokyu, the Imperial family saw the *bakufu*'s weakness as their opportunity.

From 1318 the incumbent of the throne had been the Emperor Go-Daigo, or 'Daigo the Second'. He had succeeded at the age of 30, and made it quite clear that he was a proud and ambitious man. It is difficult to tell at what stage Go-Daigo began to think of achieving his aim of absolute control by overthrowing the *bakufu,* but there is circumstantial evidence from the very beginning of his reign. On the day of his accession he sent his son, Prince Morinaga, to be a monk at Mount Hiei. There can have been no reason for removing his heir from the mainstream of politics other than to use him as a way of gaining support from the warrior monks, and this was confirmed in 1328 when he promoted Prince Morinaga to be Abbot of Mount Hiei. Prince Morinaga, an accomplished samurai warrior, is referred to as 'The Prince of the Great Pagoda' in the *Taiheiki*, the great war chronicle of the time.

In 1321 Go-Daigo abolished the hallowed tradition of the Cloistered Emperor, making clear his determination to rule directly as Emperor. Contemporary chroniclers speak well of the reforms he introduced, and contrast the lack of action the *bakufu* took against them with their speedy reaction to Go-Toba's similar attempts at independence of thought and action. There was an equally sluggish reply when the *bakufu* received hard evidence that Go-Daigo was preparing to challenge the *bakufu* rule by force. When they eventually sent an army from Kamakura, Go-Daigo had full knowledge of their approach and sufficient time to plan accordingly. As well as courting Mount Hiei he had made generous offerings to the Buddhist institutions of Nara, a wise move, considering that the *bakufu* controlled a much higher proportion of the land than had been the case under Go-Toba. In fact the governors of over half the provinces in Japan were Hojo kinsmen, so armed support from monks would be crucial.

Go-Daigo's plots were revealed to the *bakufu* in September 1331, and Go-Daigo left Kyoto for the safety of the Todai-ji in Nara. He took with him the symbols of his sovereignty – the Imperial Regalia, or at least that part of them he was able to secure. As the legitimacy of the Imperial claimant was inseparable from the question of the possession of the 'Crown Jewels', it is worth spending a little time discussing what these regalia are. They consist of three objects: the Mirror, the Sword and the Jewels. The Mirror and the Sword that are actually transmitted from one Emperor to another have been, from ancient times, replicas of the originals, which are kept respectively at Ise and the Atsuta Shrine near Nagoya. In 1185, as noted previously, this 'replica' Sword was lost at the Battle of Dan-no-Ura and, in 1210, another replica had to be made. But to all intents and purposes these replicas were treated as if they were the real thing. They were, after all, the actual objects that had passed from hand to hand as the legitimate sign of kingship. The Imperial Jewels, however, were never copied, and it was with the original Jewels, and the other 'official copies' that Go-Daigo fled to Nara.

The Todai-ji monks expressed concern that they could not withstand an attack by the *bakufu*, so Go-Daigo moved on to Kasagi, a mountain some 600 feet high overlooking the Kizugawa. It, too, was the home of warrior monks, who welcomed him and strengthened their position against an expected attack. The *bakufu* forces however first concentrated their attacks on Mount Hiei and 'The Prince of the Great Pagoda', and overcame their initially slow response to the crisis by forcing Prince Morinaga to flee for his life, thus isolating Go-Daigo at Kasagi. While the attacks continued on Kasagi, the *bakufu* made moves in the political sphere and tried to negotiate, hoping to persuade Go-Daigo to abdicate and enter a monastery.

When he refused to do so the drastic decision was made to raise another member of the Imperial family to the throne. Go-Daigo had therefore been officially deposed, but he still had the Regalia, so the actual enthronement ceremony had to be postponed until the items were recaptured.

It is at this point in the war that we first hear the name of Kusunoki Masashige, a samurai whose skill in warfare, and above all his loyalty to the legitimate Emperor, make him the model of perfection for all samurai. Little is known of his background, except that he was from an obscure warrior family in Kawachi. He suddenly enters history as Go-Daigo's staunchest supporter, and fights for him from a stronghold called Akasaka in Kawachi, a fortified encampment ('castle' is a misleading description) in the Western foothills of Mount Kongo. Here he was joined by Prince Morinaga, who helped Kusunoki defend it against a determined attack by the *bakufu*. The loyalists were short of troops and soon only the terrain frustrated the attackers' attempts. The 'castle' fell on about 20 November 1331 but, instead of making a last-ditch stand and an honourable suicide, Kusunoki Masashige and Prince Morinaga both escaped, the latter to a monastery in Nara where, according to legend, he hid in a large wooden chest. But bad news awaited them. On his way to join them in Akasaka, Go-Daigo had been captured and taken to Rokuhara, the *bakufu* headquarters in Kyoto. A few months later, in 1332, he was exiled to the island of Oki. It appeared to all that Go-Daigo's revolt had been crushed as thoroughly as that of Go-Toba, and that further resistance was useless.

Had it not been for Kusunoki Masashige and Prince Morinaga this latest attempt at Imperial restoration would indeed have been over. However, Prince Morinaga, who had by now abandoned his monkish habit and returned to the life of the son of the legitimate sovereign, based himself with an army of warrior monks in the mountainous district of Yoshino, far to the South of Kyoto, and sent out calls to arms to any samurai clans who would support him. Meanwhile his former comrade in arms, Kusunoki Masashige, continued to demonstrate how successful a continuing resistance to the *bakufu* might be. He built a new stronghold at Akasaka, Kami-Akasaka, higher up the mountain than the previous one, and inflicted such damage on the *bakufu* armies attempting to take it that orders were issued for the execution of the Prince and Kusunoki, rescinding previous commands merely for their capture.

The resistance greatly surprised the *bakufu*. Early in 1333 three armies left Kamakura to chastise the Imperial rebels. The first, commanded by a Hojo kinsman called Aso, was to attack Kami-Akasaka along the Kawachi road. The second, under Osaragi, was to attack Yoshino. Both were ultimately successful, though Kami-Akasaka only fell when its water supply was cut, and Prince Morinaga fled to Koya-san, a remote and peaceful monastery, the centre of the Shingon sect of Buddhism. The two victorious *bakufu* armies then joined the third force (under Nagoshi) for a full-scale assault on Kusunoki's newest fortification at Chihaya, to which he had withdrawn.

Chihaya was also on Mount Kongo but much stronger than Kami-Akasaka and, to the *bakufu's* amazement and chagrin, held out against every attempt to take it. The great army of the Hojo was practically immobilised in front of this makeshift mountain fortress. All of Kusunoki Masashige's skills were brought to bear in enticing the enemy to attack him in places where the terrain, with which Kusunoki's men were familiar, proved as much of a hindrance as the loyalists' arrows. Huge boulders were balanced on cliff edges, ready to be dislodged into a pass full of *bakufu* soldiers. The *bakufu* samurai were tempted into night attacks and picked off at will. Pits were dug across paths, felled trees provided almost insurmountable obstacles and, with every day that the *bakufu* spent frustrated in the forests round Chihaya, more and more samurai clans were shown that Kamakura could be challenged, and encouraged to try their hand.

In fact Chihaya was never captured and its continuing existence inspired the exiled Go-Daigo to return in the Spring of 1333. He landed in Hoki Province, on the Japan Sea coast West of Kyoto, and the local response to his return so alarmed Kamakura that the *bakufu* sent to oppose him two of their ablest generals: Nagoshi Takaie, a Hojo kinsman, and Ashikaga Takauji, who was descended from Minamoto stock and leader of one of the wealthiest families in the East.

They set out separately from Kyoto but, on his way to Hoki, Nagoshi was attacked by a guerrilla army similar to Kusunoki's under Akamatsu Norimura and was killed. His troops fled back to Kyoto, where they were absorbed by Takauji, who now had sole command of all the *bakufu* forces in Western Japan. Takauji realised what an opportunity had come his way. Unlike any other of Go-Daigo's supporters his Ashikaga family had the lineage which would enable them to accept the position of Shogun from a captive, or merely grateful, Emperor. Takauji's future lay with Go-Daigo, not the Hojo Regency. Kusunoki's defence of Chihaya was daily exposing the weakness of the Hojo state, so, declaring himself to be for the Emperor, Ashikaga Takauji turned from a pursuit of Go-Daigo and launched his army against the *bakufu's* Kyoto headquarters at Rokuhara. The surprise element was total and he succeeded in capturing the city for the rightful Emperor. Go-Daigo, still apparently in possession of the Imperial Jewels, returned in state to his throne. He generously allowed the Hojo-nominated Emperor to abdicate peacefully and retire to estates Go-Daigo made available to him, and set about restoring his previous position.

When the news of the *bakufu's* collapse in the West reached Chihaya, the siege was abandoned and many of the samurai went over to the Imperial camp. The Hojo strength was now largely confined to Eastern Japan and its doom was almost complete. In June 1333 a warrior called Nitta Yoshisada joined the Imperial supporters. He collected other opportunistic clans about him in Kozuke Province and descended from the mountains on to the *bakufu* capital of Kamakura. He divided his army into three and the columns slowly forced their way through the narrow passes that act as a natural defence for the city. Nitta Yoshisada is credited with obtaining

Samurai warrior, armed with a sword. His quiver is covered with a cloth bag to protect the arrows from rain. (From the *Gunyoki*)

Footsoldier archer, wearing a *do-maru*. (From the *Gunyoki*)

divine intervention from the Sun-Goddess, who, in response to Yoshisada's offering of his sword, caused the sea to roll back so that his army could attack Kamakura from the coastal route. After 5 days of fighting through the man-made tunnels and cuttings of Kamakura, the last of the Hojo *shikken*, along with several hundred of his men, withdrew to a small Buddhist temple, where they committed suicide as Kamakura blazed about them.

The fall of Kamakura marked the end of the Hojo Regency and the eclipse of Kamakura as the administrative capital. From now on the focus would be the Imperial capital of Kyoto. Go-Daigo's restoration of the Imperial power was complete.

Footsoldier archer, wearing a *do-maru* and carrying a bow. (From the *Gunyoki*)

43

3

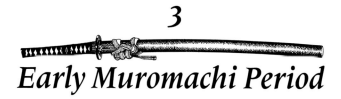

Early Muromachi Period

The return of authority to Kyoto marks the beginning of the 'Muromachi Period' in Japanese history, because the seat of the subsequent Ashikaga *bakufu* was a palace on Muromachi Avenue in Kyoto. It is convenient to subdivide this long span of time into shorter units, the first of which may be regarded as ending with the Onin War in 1467, when the capital itself was the battlefield.

The Triumph of the Ashikaga

The destruction of Kamakura in 1333 confirmed Go-Daigo as supreme ruler – for a time. The Hojo *shikken* may have disappeared for ever, but the institution of *bakufu* rule, the government of the samurai by the samurai and largely for the samurai, had attractions that only began to be appreciated once it had ended. The crisis for Go-Daigo came when he was required to make rewards to the samurai warriors who had served him so well. There were many claimants and problems of finance similar to those that had undermined the Hojo after the Mongol Wars. Many were disappointed. None had more to gain than Ashikaga Takauji, and none was more dissatisfied with his reward.

Ashikaga Takauji, as we noted in the last chapter, was of Minamoto

---

PLATE 9   *A footsoldier in a stockade in the Yoshino Mountains, 1348*

The samurai of the War Between the Courts were supported, as samurai had always been, by large numbers of footsoldiers. In this plate we see one such footsoldier taking guard from a parapet of a fortress high in the mountains of Yoshino, where the Southern Emperors held sway. His body-armour is a *hara-ate*, a very rudimentary form of protection, which consists of the front section of a samurai's *do*, without any unnecessary appendages, to which are attached three short skirt pieces, or *kusazuri*, the longer of which is central to protect the groin area. The *hara-ate* had no back-plate and was tied diagonally at the rear by stout straps, which appear to be well padded across the shoulders.

He wears two simple *kote* on his sleeves and, as it is summer, he wears a rough pair of shorts and simple, heavy cloth *suneate* or shin-protectors. Bare feet are considered adequate by this hardy warrior.

His headgear is still the traditional *eboshi* cap and the metal face-protector. His *naginata* has a particularly fierce-looking blade. The figure is based on a sketch by Sasama, and the details of the *hara-ate* on contemporary illustrations.

The great hero, Kusunoki Masashige, bids farewell to his son Masatsura as he prepares to leave to fight his last battle at Minatogawa. This poignant moment, frequently reproduced in Japanese art, is made all the more moving by the knowledge that the young boy was to follow his father in death at the Battle of Shijo-Nawate only 12 years later. This relief painting is at the Kannon-ji near Chihaya-Akasaka, and is reproduced here by kind permission of the Chief Priest.

descent, which entitled his family to the position of Shogun. In late 1335 he was ordered to re-take Kamakura, which had been recaptured in the name of the Hojo by a surviving son of the late Regent. Takauji vanquished the rebel with little difficulty but, once established in the East, his behaviour became very suspicious and, in February 1336, he was reported to be marching on Kyoto to set himself up as a new Shogun. Takauji cleverly exploited the old rivalry of the warrior monks by allying himself with Miidera, which was currently enjoying one of its periodic squabbles

This vivid oil painting of the Battle of Minatogawa was completed during the Meiji Period, when the revival of interest in Kusunoki Masashige as the archetype of loyal service to the Emperor was at its height. The painting, which is much damaged, hangs in the museum of the Minatogawa Shrine on the site of the conflict.

with Mount Hiei. But his attempt was not a success. His advance Westwards was opposed by various loyalists and the Mount Hiei monks, and Takauji was defeated. He was driven out of the capital and pursued as far as the narrow straits that divide Honshu from Kyushu, where he was forced to cross to the Southern island for support.

In the majority of cases in samurai history such a severe defeat proves total, but Ashikaga began to play upon the grievances of Kyushu samurai against their contemporaries on Honshu. Some local clans eventually rallied behind him and his numbers swelled greatly after a victory at the Battle of Tadara Beach. By early June 1336 Ashikaga Takauji felt sufficiently confident to return to Honshu.

The advance of the Ashikaga host by sea and by land caused panic in the Court, and a fearful Go-Daigo ordered a stand to be made at the Minato River, where it flows into the sea at the present-day city of Kobe. Nitta Yoshisada had already taken his stand here to await the enemy, but Kusunoki Masashige warned Go-Daigo that to attempt to fight a pitched battle would lead to disaster. He suggested instead that Go-Daigo should leave Kyoto for Mount Hiei and its loyal monks, while Kusunoki conducted a campaign of harassment against the Ashikaga in much the same way that he had kept the *bakufu* forces at bay on Mount Kongo. These tactics had worked before, but one gets the impression that Go-Daigo's victory had made him much less inclined to flee from place to

47

place. The Court, with Go-Daigo's support, refused to accept Kusunoki's suggestion. They were decided upon a battle and, not wishing to take issue with the Emperor whom he had served so loyally, Masashige had no choice but to agree, and rode off to share in what he knew would be an inevitable defeat.

The Battle of Minatogawa

The Battle of Minatogawa took place on a hot, humid day. Kusunoki took a stand with his back to the Minato River against the advance of Takauji's son, Tadayoshi. The seaborne force, under Hosokawa, attempted to land to the loyalists' rear to cut off their retreat. Kusunoki's resistance was fierce and the battle could have gone either way, had it not been for a fatal error of judgement on the part of Nitta Yoshisada, who withdrew from the front line when Hosokawa succeeded in landing at his rear. Soon Nitta was driven from the field and the whole of the Ashikaga army closed in around Kusunoki Masashige. He committed suicide as soon as it was seen that the day was hopeless. It is interesting to note that, on several occasions before, Masashige had been defeated and returned to fight another day. Why was Minatogawa different? Why had the loss of Kami-Akasaka not obliged him to commit suicide to atone for his failure? The answer lies in the notion of samurai loyalty. In the campaigns around Mount Kongo it had been the will of the Emperor that Masashige should keep on fighting, fleeing from mountain to mountain. That was the nature of the loyal service that was required of him. But at Minatogawa such a course of action had been ruled out, and it was the inevitable consequence of the Emperor's decision that Masashige should fight to the last.

PLATE 10   *A samurai in leather-covered armour with a* no-dachi, *ca 1410*

The bitter days of the early fifteenth century are recalled in this plate, which illustrates armour contemporary with the murder of the Shogun Ashikaga Yoshinori by Akamatsu Mitsusuke (1388–1441).

This unusual leather-covered armour, the original of which is in the Tokyo National Museum, shows a perfectly logical development of armour in which all the outer surfaces of the plates, except the bottom one, were covered in a sheet of leather to protect the individual cords underneath. In a sense this style anticipates the more rigid solid plates that were to make their appearance in the following century.

The armour has a sombre, workaday appearance, and must have had much less flexibility than the traditional styles. The old *sendan-no-ita* and *kyubi-no-ita* of the *yoroi* have been replaced by two small appendages that are merely functional, and cover the cords that fasten the armour together on the collar bones against a sword stroke. Note the large *sode* still being worn, and the adoption of two armoured sleeves, any pretence of being a mounted archer having been completely discarded. His shin-guards are big and clumsy, and he has obviously decided that he has no need of *haidate*.

His helmet is quite remarkable. The wide sweeping *shikoro* has reached its ultimate level, being almost horizontal (of. Plates 7 and 8), making the wearer include an additional, smaller set of leather(?) plates closer to the head.

His wicked-looking long sword is a *no-dachi*, which augments his *katana* and *tanto* in his belt. The *no-dachi*, which resembles a *naginata* more than it does a sword, was carried in a long scabbard over the shoulder. One of the characters in the famous film *The Seven Samurai* has a *no-dachi* as his preferred weapon, though his is not as large as this example, which is authentic.

He died as a true samurai, which is how he is remembered, motivated entirely by loyalty to the Emperor, in complete contrast to the machinations of Ashikaga Takauji, whose motives were solely ones of self-interest and the advancement of his family. This, at any rate, is how Kusunoki and Ashikaga have been represented throughout history, and there is no other samurai who can better represent the ideals of the warrior than Kusunoki Masashige.

The Emperors of Yoshino

Ashikaga Takauji, of course, had a different prize from that of immortality. It was to his family that the title of Shogun was to pass, but there was some more bitter fighting before he could be assured of his triumph. Takauji thus became the first Ashikaga Shogun. He had first-hand experience of the remoteness of Kamakura when independent-minded Emperors were abroad, so Takauji took the administrative seat of military government back to the home of the Imperial family and set up his headquarters in the Muromachi district of Kyoto.

After Minatogawa, Go-Daigo was forced to take refuge on Mount Hiei, just as Kusunoki had originally suggested. Takauji turned all his forces on to this mountain stronghold and, according to the chronicles, was only able to secure the person of Go-Daigo by means of trickery, as the *sohei* fought savagely. There were tricks on both sides, however, for Go-Daigo's supporters were to claim for the next half century that the Regalia which Go-Daigo surrendered to Takauji, and which were thereupon used for the enthronement of the Ashikaga nominee, the Emperor Kogon, were in fact counterfeit. Go-Daigo thus maintained that, even though he had been deposed for a second time, he was still the rightful Emperor and, in fact, made explicit statements of it in various written communications. In 1337 he frustrated the Ashikaga by managing to escape from custody to the mountains of Yoshino, where he and his successors were to reign as rival Emperors until 1392. The cherry-tree clad hills of Yoshino had been the temporary refuge of Prince Morinaga and had a terrain ideally suited to defence. Go-Daigo also discovered that he had considerable support, notably from the survivors of the Kusunoki family. Masatsura, Masashige's son, carried on the fight after his father's death until he was cut down at the Battle of Shijo-Nawate in 1348.

Go-Daigo died in 1339. Prince Morinaga had pre-deceased him, so his younger son, Prince Norinaga, became the second 'Southern Emperor' Fighting between the two lines continued around the country till 1392, but towards the end many of the combatants had forgotten why they were fighting and changed allegiance from 'Northern' to 'Southern' Court whenever it suited their personal aspirations to do so. The lines were finally united under the third Ashikaga Shogun, Yoshimitsu, a skilled politician who organised trade with China and enjoyed the respect of all. It is to Yoshimitsu that we owe the building of the famous 'Golden Pavilion' which symbolised the glory of the Ashikaga, but his greatest achievement occurred in 1392 when he persuaded the rival Emperors to reconcile their differences and proposed a scheme whereby Go-Kameyama, the Southern Emperor, would abandon his claim to the throne in return for a guarantee that the succession would then alternate between the two lines. Go-Kameyama agreed, and the war ended, but in fact the mechanism of alternation was never put into operation. In 1412 the Northern Emperor, Go-Komatsu, abdicated in favour of his son, Shoko (1401–1428), and, when the latter died, the succession passed to another Northern Emperor, Go-Hanazono (1419–1470). Go-Kameyama's son, Prince Ogura, claimed his right to the throne, but was ignored by the Ashikaga *bakufu*, who had no intention of honouring the agreement. In fact there was never to be another 'Southern Emperor', and the Northern Court has provided every Emperor down to the present day.

Even though the reconciliation provided a much-needed peace, the supporters of the Yoshino Emperors knew they had been cheated and, no less than three times in the next century, stubborn loyalists to the Southern Court attempted to restart the war, using the line of 'Southern Pretenders' which Prince Ogura was to produce. The first revolt, in 1413, was led by Kitabatake Mitsumasa on behalf of Prince Ogura himself, but the move was soon crushed. In 1428, with the accession of Go-Hanazono, Kitabatake tried again, supported by the latest in a long line of Kusunoki samurai, Mitsumasa. The plot involved assassinating the fifth Ashikaga Shogun, Yoshinori, but the scheme was discovered and Kusunoki was beheaded in 1429. The third, and final, attempt proved much more successful and, although a little known incident in Japanese history, it adds its own bizarre appendix to the story of Go-Daigo and the tales of samurai loyalty.

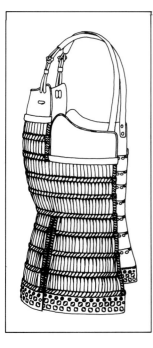

A *hara-ate*
A type of body armour, protecting only the torso and groin, suspended from cords at the shoulders. It was used by footsoldiers between *c.*1300 and 1550.

The Heavenly King

By the fourth decade of the fifteenth century the Ashikaga Shogunate was entering a period of decline. Yoshimitsu had set it on a glittering peak of achievement, which his successors Yoshimochi and Yoshikazu consolidated, and it appeared that the sixth Shogun, Yoshinori, was also destined for glory. Yoshinori's end came, however, when he tried to curtail the growing power of the Akamatsu clan by transferring some territories from the then head of the clan, Mitsusuke (1381–1441), to Yoshinori's homosexual lover, Akamatsu Sadamura, a kinsman of Mitsusuke and his rival for clan leadership. To forestall this measure, Mitsusuke plotted the Shogun's death and, in the summer of 1441, invited Yoshinori to a celebration at his Kyoto mansion to mark the Akamatsu's recent defeat of the Yuki clan. The unsuspecting Shogun accepted the invitation and, when the party was at its height, two Akamatsu retainers released all the horses from the stables into the garden, where they kicked and bit each other and created a great uproar. Under cover of the confusion the Akamatsu samurai set on the Shogun and relieved him of his head. The assassins then calmly withdrew from Kyoto to their territories in Harima, leaving behind them (according to the chronicler of this so-called 'Kakitsu Affair') 'none to disembowel themselves and none to pursue', suggesting that the Akamatsu were not alone in their plotting. It was 3 days before a force could be assembled to ride off to bring them to justice, and even then the expeditionary force hesitated at the provincial border. Yamana Sozen (1404–1474) was the only samurai leader who decided to 'break ranks' and advance against the rebels, and was rewarded by being granted the Akamatsu's territories of Harima, Bizen and Mimasaka.

Yoshinori was succeeded by his son Yoshikatsu, who succeeded at the age of 8 and died at the age of 10, to be followed by his younger brother Yoshimasa, also 8 years old. Yoshimasa enjoyed a long 30-year reign as Shogun, filled with many aesthetic advances, much of which was to be offset by the virtual collapse of Shogunal authority. However, to return to the death of Yoshinori, one group that took advantage of the Akamatsu's appalling crime was the Southern Court adherents, then under the leadership of a certain Hino Arimitsu. On 16 October 1443, they broke into the Imperial Palace, set fire to some buildings and, in the confusion, made off with two items of Regalia, the replica Sword and the Jewels. They were hotly pursued and the Sword was recaptured after a skirmish near the Kiyomizu temple. They succeeded in presenting the Jewels to the heir of the Southern Court, Prince Takayoshi, sometimes known as Prince Manju-ji, who was living under the protection of the *sohei* of Mount Hiei. (There is in fact some confusion as to who the actors in this drama actually were. The 'Young Pretender' is referred to elsewhere as Prince Takahide. Other accounts credit the raid on the palace to Kusunoki Jiro Masahide, of whom little is known.) The immediate result of their efforts was a *bakufu* attack on Mount Hiei, which resulted in the Pretender's death. The Jewels were

---

PLATE 11 *A samurai, wearing a* haramaki, *enters a village, ca 1440*

This rear view of a group of samurai entering a village shows several points of detail about armour which are relevant from about 1440 to 1500. The helmet is of multi-plate construction, with a wide *shikoro*, though not so grotesquely so as Plate 10. His body armour is a *haramaki*, and the rear view shows the separate *kusazuri* that make it so different from a *yoroi*. This particular style of armour fastened down the middle of the back. The fastenings cannot be seen because they are concealed under the separate plate known as

the *sei-ita*, referred to sometimes, for obvious reasons, as the 'coward's plate'. Tied to the ring of the *sei-ita* is an *agemaki* bow, which still performs its traditional function of holding the *sode* (the shoulder-plates) in place. As the *sode* are much smaller, and contoured to the arm, there seems little need for the *agemaki*, and in time its use will become purely decorative, until it disappears altogether with the invention of the *sashimono*, the identification flag worn at the back of armour, the carrier for which leaves no room for

an *agemaki*.

He wears two *kote*, as is now universal, and also wears a strange form of *haidate* (thigh-guards), which are basically armour-plated shorts! His *suneate* are still quite large, but the wearing of ordinary straw sandals, rather than any specialised footwear, is now standard.

His sword is suspended *tachi*-style, with the cutting edge downwards, as it has always been, and he has a *tanto* tied securely above it. His main weapon, however, is a *naginata*.

Site of the final resistance to the Northern Court, Sannoko Canyon, deep within the mountains of Yoshino, was the hiding place for the Imperial Regalia taken by supporters of the Southern Emperors in 1443. They managed to hold out for 14 years.

taken away by the Kusunoki family to Yoshino where they proclaimed the Pretender's son, Prince Kitayama, as Emperor (referring to him as 'The Heavenly King') and set up his brother Tadayoshi as Shogun.

This dramatic raid was a serious challenge to the Ashikaga *bakufu*'s declining authority, for as we have seen before, great store was laid on the legitimacy provided by the possession of the Regalia. The Shogunate rallied its support and fierce attacks forced the Southern Court to retreat from Yoshino, deeper into the forested mountains around Mount Odaigahara, where they raised a palace for the 'Heavenly King', and hid the Jewels in a cave. From here this 'unofficial' Southern Court managed to hold out for another 14 years.

Their eventual defeat was almost as theatrical as their initial success. The Akamatsu clan had been in disgrace since the murder of Yoshinori, but the Shogun Yoshimasa made it clear that they would be restored to favour if they destroyed the Southern Court. Some retainers of the Akamatsu therefore made the dangerous journey to the Sannoko River, where the rebels had their base, and presented themselves as sympathisers come to join their cause. As the Akamatsu were the former destroyers of a Shogun the loyalists were completely fooled. One night the new arrivals turned on their host and slew the Southern Emperor (who was either the former Prince Kitayama referred to above, or a successor called Takamasa), then made off in two groups through the snow, one with his head and the other with the Jewels. Legend adds a colourful touch to their escape, for as the group with the head, under Nakamura Taroshiro, were crossing the Obagamine Pass they were attacked by samurai from Yoshino. They buried the Emperor's head in the snow, meaning to retrieve it afterwards, but in the midst of the fighting the head sent up a spurt of blood and the loyalists were able to recapture it. The Jewels, however, were safely returned to the capital.

That was the end of the Southern Court. During the Onin War of 1467–77 the Yamana clan briefly displayed a 'Southern Emperor' to offset the Hosokawa's manipulation of the Emperor Go-Tsuchimikado, but found no Kusunoki to support him, and from then on such figures disappear from history. However, as a footnote to the story of the *Nambokucho* or 'Wars

---

PLATE 12   *A samurai, wielding an iron club, fights in the Onin War in 1467*

The Onin War, which began in the First Year of Onin, 1467, and lasted intermittently for another 10 years, marked the final collapse of the Ashikaga Shogunate as an institution with any real power, and the emergence of a number of land-owning *daimyo* who ruled their provinces with little regard for anything beyond their own immediate concerns. The Onin War began in the city of Kyoto, where rival samurai clans burnt each other's mansions and fought street battles. This plate attempts to illustrate these unhappy early days.

The samurai, whose appearance is based almost entirely on a sketch by Sasama, wears a *do-maru* armour, which opens at the right side, and is otherwise almost identical to a *haramaki*. His *sode* have a gentle curve, and are of medium size, so they would probably be anchored to an *agemaki* at the rear. Two small metal plates protect the suspensory cords on the chest, as in Plate 10, and he also sports a sensible innovation, the *nodowa*, or throat-protector, which fastened round the neck and hung in front of the neck. His *do* has seven *kusazuri*. His helmet is of similar style to the one with the wide-sweeping neckguard shown in Plate 10, but he has eschewed *kuwagata*, and his long black hair hangs down inside it. His helmet cords are twisted securely around his chin.

A long belt, the *uwa-obi*, pulls the loose *do-maru* into his waist, taking some of the weight off the shoulders. This problem of the distribution of the armour's weight was only solved by the introduction of a tapered waist in the sixteenth century. His *kote* are surprisingly modern. Gone are the simple cloth bags to which plates have been sewn. Instead we see an early form of chain-mail protection, which was to become universal during the following century. The metal plates are fastened with thongs. His *haidate* are similar to those seen from the rear in Plate 11, and his heavy metal *suneate* complete what is a good example of plain, undecorative, fifteenth-century battledress.

He is certainly taking no chances with personal armament, having two *tanto* (daggers) in addition to his sword. His main weapon is, however, an enormous studded iron club, with which he appears to have caused havoc!

Between the Courts', we may mention that in 1945 no less than seventeen 'Pretenders' claimed to be the rightful Emperor and objected to Hirohito's surrender to the United States of America. One man, a shopkeeper from Nagoya called Kumazawa Kando, who claimed to be descended from the Southern line, attracted a great deal of attention and even came to the notice of General MacArthur. Some are still around. A new religious sect in Japan owes its allegiance to a lady who claims to be descended from the rightful line. In her case, however, she goes further than rejecting the settlement of 1392 and claims descent from Susano-o, the thunder God, the Goddess Amateratsu's elder brother and thus the founder of the real line of Emperors of which she is the first claimant!

The Kongo-ji in Kashiwagi, at the head of the Kono Valley, is the traditional site of the palace of the rival Shogun, the younger brother of the last of the 'Southern Pretenders', whose tomb appears in this picture. The destruction of the remnants of the Southern Court proved the means whereby the Akamatsu clan was restored to favour after the Kakitsu Incident, when the Shogun Yoshinori was murdered.

The Onin War

Ashikaga Yoshimitsu, who had united the Imperial lines, had built a

58

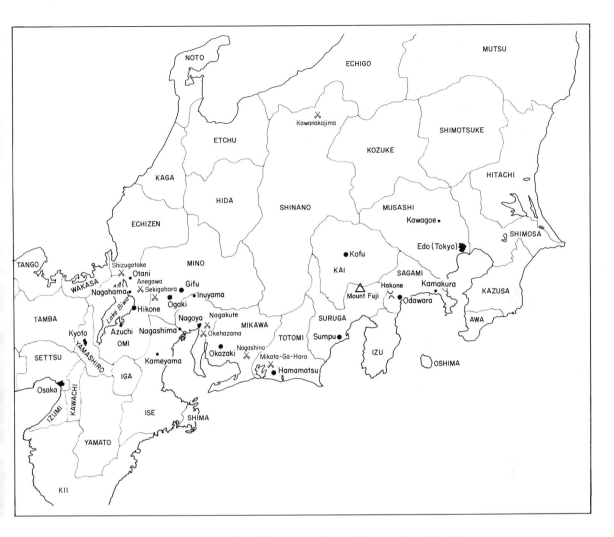

Central Honshu, showing the provinces that lay between Kyoto and Edo (Tokyo), major battlefields and towns. The major landowning daimyo are shown in the territories they controlled in the latter half of the sixteenth century.

Pavilion of Gold. His grandson, the aesthete Yoshimasa, was to attempt to emulate him by constructing a Silver Pavilion in 1483, and wept when the troubled times made it impossible to finish the work, so that the building stood gaunt and black, as fitting a symbol of the new age as the glorious gold had been of a previous generation.

Between the times of building of the Gold and the Silver Pavilions, the samurai had fought the war named after the Year of Onin in which it had begun. What began as a succession dispute between samurai clans turned into a fragmented civil war. Even a nation so used to violence found the Onin War particularly terrible, for the city of Kyoto was its first battlefield, where bands of samurai challenged each other from among the blackened ruins of what had once been houses, shops and temples. Peasant riots and armed monks had brought their own destruction in the past, but attacks like these ended as precipitately as they arrived. During the war of Onin the agony went on and on, with no respite over 10 years for the rebuilding of homes and the reconstruction of a shattered society. Only the eventual spread of the war to distant provinces ultimately gave Kyoto the breathing space it needed. The merchants and craftsmen returned, the temples were rebuilt once again, and the cycle of death and rebirth went on.

Three of the clans mentioned previously in this chapter became prominent by their involvement in the Onin War. Within 10 years of the Akamatsu's restoration of fortune by defeating the Heavenly King they took part in the bitter conflict. Akamatsu Masanori (1455–1496) was a well-known general. He was the grandson of Akamatsu Mitsusuke, the murderer of the Shogun Yoshinori. The Yamana, who had profited by their revenge of Shogun Yoshinori's death, were represented in the Onin War by the same Yamana Mochitoyo, known by his Buddhist name of 'Sozen', and nicknamed the 'Red Monk' because of his fiery complexion. The Red Monk's chief enemy was his son-in-law, Hosokawa Katsumoto, showing that clan issues as such over-rode all humanitarian considerations. All that mattered was survival. Hostages were given for good behaviour and frequently met an untimely end.

By the end of the Onin War in 1477 the power of the Shogun as a military force had collapsed entirely. He was now honoured as a figurehead, as an Emperor without the attendant divinity, respected only for the legitimacy of the Imperial commission-to-rule which only a family descended from the Minamoto could possess. Real power now lay elsewhere, as new families replaced old ones. There had been strong, independent samurai clans before, but precious few managed to make the transition from

---

PLATE 13   *Hosokawa Sumimoto leads a charge, ca 1510*

We enter the sixteenth century with Hosokawa Sumimoto (1496–1520), whose life bears so many of the hallmarks of the Sengoku Period – the Age of the Country at War. His father, Hosokawa Masamoto (1466-1507), was the son of the great general, Katsumoto, who fought in the Onin War. In 1493 he acted as kingmaker and deposed the rightful Shogun Ashikaga Yoshitane. Masamoto was childless, and adopted three sons to carry on the Hosokawa name. This Sumimoto was the second of the three, and was only 11 years old when his adoptive father died. A dispute broke out almost immediately and young Sumimoto took refuge with the Sasaki family in Omi Province. The powerful Miyoshi Nagateru supported Sumimoto and disposed of his elder 'brother', Sumiyuki. This enabled Sumimoto to take possession of the domains intended

for him on Shikoku Island and attain the high office of Kwanryo in Kyoto. His triumphs were soon put into reverse when the Shogun, whom his father had deposed, returned to Kyoto under the protection of Ouchi Yoshioki. Hosokawa Sumimoto intended to stop him in Settsu Province but, seeing the size of his army, fled to Shikoku. Ouchi Yoshioki entered Kyoto, restored the Shogun and took Sumimoto's title of Kwanryo. Sumimoto's eventual return marked the beginning of a series of battles between him and the Shogun's supporters, which eventually ended in Sumimoto's defeat and final withdrawal to Shikoku, where he died in 1520.

In this plate Sumimoto is seen leading a desperate charge across a rice-field. His *do-maru* is almost identical to the one shown in Plate 12, but his helmet has a deeper *shikoro*, making it look almost old-

fashioned. His *nodowa* is unusual in that he has tucked it under the top of his *do*. His *sode* are large, and would be tied at the rear via an *agemaki* bow similar to that depicted in Plate 11. His armour is completely laced in black except for the bottom row of his *haidate*. His *suneate*, which are of a russet-iron finish, are very large indeed.

Two items proclaim his status as a commander: his whip, slung casually across his *tanto*, and his signalling fan. There were several varieties of these. Sumimoto has a flat wooden one called a *gumbai uchiwa*, which was reserved for commanders. Note that horse furniture has not changed appreciably over the centuries.

The source for these details is a contemporary painting on silk of Hosokawa Sumimoto in a private collection in Japan.

Shogun's man before the Onin War to their own man after it. Some, like the Shimazu in the far South of Kyushu, achieved it with the help of their geographical remoteness from the capital. Other noble houses died out as completely as their burned mansions that had once graced the Kyoto skyline. Yamana, Isshiki and Hatakeyama disappeared from history. Takeda, Uesugi and Saito, the new *daimyo*, or 'warlords', who replaced them, were almost invariably lower-class opportunists who had seized the moment and made the transfer of power a reality for themselves.

The wars that followed Onin became spread throughout the country in a very different way from the war between the Courts. There were no sides to choose in these wars, just the terrible realisation that every clan had to fight to survive. Smaller clans allied themselves with larger until they were able to confront their erstwhile protectors. Ambitious leaders of samurai put more and more men into battle, so that even the despised peasants were given spears and swords to fight with beside the samurai élite and were called *ashigaru*, or 'light feet', because the leaders could not afford armour for them. Soon the most ignorant village blacksmith had become a swordmaker, mass-producing spear heads for the samurai and crude swords for the *ashigaru*, so that the quality of work plummeted to a crude and shameful level. The poorly-tempered, brittle blades shattered against armour and such was the mistrust placed in these inferior swords that a samurai forced by poverty to depend upon them would take five or six with him into battle, ready to be discarded at will. The glory of the Ashikaga, and its most potent symbol, the peerless samurai sword, were both passing away.

4

Sengoku Period – the Age of the Country at War

In view of the number of battles we have described in the preceding pages the dubbing of the years from 1477 to 1576 as the *Sengoku-jidai* or 'Age of the Country at War' may seem an unnecessary appellation to give to any one time in Japanese history. The reason this latter half of the Muromachi Period is so-called, however, is better explained by a more exact translation of the term. Sengoku-jidai is in fact a way of making a direct comparison between the condition of Japan at the time and the 'Period of Warring States' in Ancient China. Unlike the Wars Between the Courts, and the Gempei War, there was no real conflict over Shogunal or Imperial authority – such a centralised power simply did not exist. Both institutions continued but, as noted in the previous chapter, real power lay elsewhere. The wars of the Sengoku Period were fought between contingents representing two different sorts of military grouping: the *daimyo*, or samurai warlords, and the peasant leagues, or *ikki*.

The Army of the Holy Lotus

As we have seen on several previous occasions any apparent weakening of Shogunal authority was a signal to other groups to try their hand. More

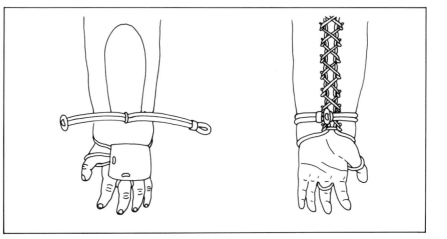

Armour for the sleeve
The means of attaching the *kote* (armoured sleeve) to the hand changed little through the centuries in spite of changes in the *kote* design. There was a loop round the wrist, fastened with toggles, and two smaller loops, one around the thumb, and another around the middle finger.

than Emperors were willing to challenge the Shogunate after the Kakitsu Affair, the murder of the Shogun Yoshinori in 1441. This not only provided a stimulus for the Southern Court supporters to try their last desperate attempt at power, but also provided the ideal conditions of confusion in Kyoto to enable peasant rioters, in leagues called *ikki*, to descend with impunity upon the capital, a trend that is first discerned in the mid-fifteenth century, but reaches its peak in the confusion following the Onin War.

The grievances of country-dwellers after Onin were directed against the rich pawnbrokers and rice-dealers of the city who had grown fat at the farmers' expense. As the finances of these *doso*, or merchants, were indispensable to the humble shopkeepers and artisans who lived beside them no support was found for the peasants among their urban counterparts. Instead there grew up a strong measure of urban solidarity against the peasant *ikki* and, as the *bakufu* became increasingly unable or unwilling to defend them against such incursions, this solidarity took the form of armed intervention. This military resistance to the *ikki* was in fact the beginning of a heady period of virtual self-government for the people of Kyoto. More than occupation divided them from the rural *ikki*, for their religious differences were paramount. The esoteric sects of Buddhism, such as the Tendai of the warrior monks of Mount Hiei, had made little headway with the simple-minded townsfolk. Their mainstay was the sect founded by the monk Nichiren, known either by the name of its founder, or as the *Hokke-*

PLATE 14   *Yamamoto Kansuke prepares to join in the Fourth Battle of Kawanakajima, 1561*

Yamamoto Kansuke takes us into the most exciting period of samurai history, the *Sengoku-jidai*, the 'Age of the Country at War'. The one-eyed Kansuke was a trusted advisor to the great *daimyo* Takeda Shingen (1521–1573) and one of the Takeda's renowned 'Twenty-Four Generals'. Takeda Shingen and his arch-rival, Uesugi Kenshin, fought five battles in the flat plain of Kawanakajima, near the present-day city of Nagano in Nagano Prefecture. This plate is based on the most famous of these encounters, which was fought in 1561.

We are standing on the hills overlooking Shingen's fortress of Kaizu (now Matsushiro) down in the valley. The battle has begun across the Chikuma-gawa towards Hachiman Plain. Kansuke's personal retainers begin the descent towards the conflict. Their *sashimono*, the little flags on their backs, are characteristic of the period now

under discussion. They bear Kansuke's *mon*, or badge, which is also seen in modified form as a *maedate*, the badge on the front of his helmet. When the battle was joined, Yamamoto Kansuke created havoc in the Uesugi ranks by charging singlehanded with his long spear, an act that almost certainly saved the Takeda from a crushing defeat. Eventually, overcome by wounds from arquebus fire, Kansuke retired and committed *hara-kiri*. (For a full, detailed account of the Battle of Kawanakajima see *Battles of the Japanese Samurai* by the present author.)

His helmet is an excellent example of the way a simple 'battle-dress' suit of armour, so typical of the age, could be made to look spectacular. This helmet is one of several known from the sixteenth century that sported enormous wooden buffalo horns. (Kuroda Nagamasa possessed the best-known example,

which is illustrated in Plate 25. See also the author's *The Samurai – a Military History* for the one owned by Tokugawa Ieyasu.) Similar basic helmets will be noted in most of the plates that follow, but the reader will appreciate the tremendous difference in overall design between this and preceding illustrations. The *fukigayeshi* have shrunk to small projections, and the *shikoro* is very simple. Note the very basic *hoate*, a face-mask, which at this stage of development is little more than an anchoring plate for the helmet cords. As Kansuke was a Buddhist monk, like Shingen, he wears the monk's *kesa* over his armour. The rear view of the armour would be very similar to those illustrated in Plate 27.

The sources for the illustration are materials displayed in the museums at Kawanakajima and Matsushiro, and numerous contemporary illustrations.

shu, or Lotus sect, from the fundamental importance Nichiren attached to the teachings enshrined within the Lotus Sutra. By about 1500 there were twenty-one Nichiren temples in Kyoto, several of which were very sensibly surrounded by moats and earthen embankments for protection.

By placing their reliance on their own efforts the craftsmen and merchants of Kyoto had clearly rejected the traditional role of the samurai to protect them, and formed their own self-governing, self-defending organisations that had as little regard for class or pedigree as had the new *daimyo* of the distant provinces. United in their need for protection, and inspired by their brash, tub-thumping Buddhism, these townsmen armies made the samurai of the Shogun seem archaic in their obsession with rank, honour and the self-destructive demands of samurai glory.

Their biggest challenge came in 1528. Not even the presence of townsmen armies could dissuade the Shogun from fleeing before the advance of a huge army on Kyoto. It was not an army of samurai as the Shogun understood the term – there was no pedigree to inspect, no worthy opponents to challenge. Nor was it a rabble of *sohei* monks from one of the old monasteries of Nara or Mount Hiei, who had attacked the city in the past. It was instead the first united attack upon Kyoto by the Ikko-ikki, or 'Single-minded League', adherents of the Jodo-Shinshu sect of Buddhism, who believed that death in battle guaranteed heaven, while retreat promised eternal damnation.

An armour of *haramaki* style, which opens down the middle of the back. It has a large *nodowa,* the protector for the throat, and curved shoulder-plates, or *sode.*

The Rise of the Ikko-ikki

It is a mistake to think of the Ikko-ikki as warrior monks analogous to the *sohei* of Mount Hiei. They were rather more of a social movement, far more developed than the ordinary *ikki,* with a religious basis uniting them even more fiercely than the townsmen's Nichiren sect. Some may have shaved their heads, but the majority dressed, fought and died like the samurai they opposed. Jodo-Shinshu, the sect to which the Ikko belonged, which is today the largest Buddhist denomination in Japan, was an offshoot of the Jodo, or 'Pure Land' sect, and placed its faith in the Vow of Amida Buddha to save all mankind, rather than restricting salvation to those with the leisure and the intellect to explore the spirituality of the esoteric creeds such as the Tendai of Mount Hiei. Jodo-Shinshu was given a much-needed revival under Rennyo (1415–1499), who succeeded in uniting the many diverse independent groups of adherents (known as *monto,* hence the alternative name for the Ikko as the Monto sect) under his leadership.

The emergence of the Ikko-ikki as a military force reached its consummation with their conquest of the province of Kaga in 1488, a territory they managed to hold until 1580. Such political power inevitably encouraged a shift from the collective, egalitarian organisation they had been, whereby oaths were signed in a circle so that no one took precedence over another. On some occasions these *ikki* documents were then burned, the

Samurai, wearing armour typical of the mid-sixteenth century, attack a house.

ashes dissolved in water, and the resulting liquid drunk by the confederates. By the middle of the sixteenth century the Ikko-ikki form of organisation had become largely indistinguishable from that other form of collective security: the *daimyo* domain, the territory of a warlord. As noted above, unlike the townsmen's Lotus sect, their support came from the country-side, where disaffected peasants saw in the salvation promised by Shinshu, and the more earthly benefits conveyed by the Ikko-ikki, a splendid alter-native to service to any samurai family, new or old. By 1520 they controlled three provinces from their huge fortress of Ishiyama Hongan-ji in Osaka, which they defended with an army as formidable as any of the *daimyo,* and it was only a matter of time before they turned their attentions to the rich pickings of the newly prosperous Kyoto.

In their 1528 campaign they had, however, reckoned without the resourceful townspeople of Kyoto. As the army of the Ikko-ikki approach-ed the capital, the army of the Hokke-shu began to mobilise with a rapidity which would have astonished even samurai. Swords, armour and banners appeared from nowhere, and for weeks a force of thousands paraded through the streets under the flag of Nichiren, chanting the Lotus Sutra. The Ikko-ikki were driven off. There then began a successful, if somewhat grudging, alliance between the 'Old Guard' of the samurai class and their fellow human beings outside it. In 1533 the Lotus army joined forces with Hosokawa Harumoto (1519–1563) for an attack on the Ikko-ikki's huge 'fortress cathedral' of the Ishiyama Hongan-ji, which stood on the site of present-day Osaka castle. So secure did their joint efforts make Kyoto that the Shogun Yoshiharu returned in 1534 to the city from which he had fled in 1528 and, within months, the gardens of the Shogun's Palace rang once again to the sound of music and song.

But the peace was illusory. The townsmen of the Hokke-shu had been altogether too successful in filling the temporary vacuum of authority which existed in Kyoto. Their intolerant religious fundamentalism, as much as their assertion of proprietorial rights, particularly offended the monks of Mount Hiei. After securing the neutrality of the townsmen's erstwhile ally, Hosokawa Harumoto, and the approval of the Ikko-ikki at Ishiyama Hongan-ji, the *sohei* of Mount Hiei descended in a surprise attack on the city with a ferocity that they had not even exercised at the height of the Gempei War. All twenty-one Nichiren temples were burned to the ground and the conflagration took much of the rest of the city with it. Thus one of the forms of social organisation which had emerged out of the ashes of the Onin War came to a violent end. The self-governing structure of Kyoto lasted a few more years after the destruction of its Nichiren nuclei, until it was all swept aside in the triumph of Oda Nobunaga. The Ikko-ikki shared in the victory, but it was the other trend mentioned briefly above, the *daimyo* domain, that really prospered. As it was a *daimyo* who was to to bring about the Ikko-ikki's downfall it is to this final manifestation of Sengoku military power that we must now turn.

The Warlords of Western Japan

The development of the *daimyo* is best illustrated by tracing the careers of

---

PLATE 15   *The war-drum of the Takeda summons the troops, c. 1564*

The most important signalling devices in any army were the war-drums. This is the particularly large version which would be mounted in a drum-tower of a castle. A burly *ashigaru*, or footsoldier, hammers out the call to war for the Takeda clan. He is wearing the most straightforward of all 'battle-dress' armours, the *okegawa-do*, which consists of two sections, front and back, connected by a hinge and fastening under the right armpit by a cord. The *kusazuri* (or *gesan*), the tassels that hang down over the thighs, are of simple construction laced in *sugake-odoshi* (paired cords). Many samurai armours of the period are nothing more than ornamented *okegawa-do*s.

Drumming is hot work – so the drummer has dispensed with all other items of clothing except for his *fundoshi*, or loincloth, which is visible through the cords of his *kusazuri*.

The castle may look a rudimentary construction to those who are familiar with pictures of the stone structures of Himeji and Hikone, but this is the authentic style of the period. Some stone was used, but the vast sweeping stone walls of Odawara and Edo would not be found in the mountains of Kai Province. Nor did Takeda Shingen prefer to place great reliance on castles. The loyal people of his province were his castle. Wood is therefore the main material of this typical mid-sixteenth century fortress.

Ascending the stairs behind the drummer comes a member of Takeda Shingen's *tsukai-ban*, or messenger corps, an army unit maintained by every *daimyo* of note. 'Aide-de-camp' is probably the best translation. The Takeda aides-de-camp were distinguished by the very appropriate device of a busy centipede on their *sashimono*. Behind him comes a samurai who wears the *sashimono* of one of Shingen's greatest generals, Baba Nobuharu, who was to meet his death at the cataclysmic Battle of Nagashino in 1575. The flags of some other Takeda generals' troops are seen down in the courtyard. There are the six black rings on red of Sanada Yukitaka, the first of the Sanada to serve Shingen; the Takeda *mon* on blue of Takeda Nobukado, Shingen's brother; the red octagon on white of Obata Masamori; the black zig-zag of Baba; the black design on white of Hara Masatane, who was to be killed during the charge at Nagashino, and the white flower on black of another victim of Nagashino – Yamagata Masakage.

The sources for the heraldic designs are materials collected by the author from Kofu in Yamanashi Prefecture, which was formerly Shingen's capital. Every year local people dress up in authentic costume for the 'Shingen-ko matsuri', to commemorate the district's most famous son.

representative examples, and history provides us with many from which we can choose. The Western end of Honshu furnishes us with the case of how the ancient clan of Ouchi were overthrown by the Mori in a classic case of *gekokujo*, 'the low overcome the high', which is the phrase used to describe how one *daimyo*, often of a highly prestigious family, might be overcome by his inferiors, who could even be his own samurai.

The Ouchi had an impressive pedigree, claiming descent from a Korean prince who came to Japan in 611, and the record of their achievements reads like a potted history of Japan. Ouchi Hiroyo was one of the many samurai leaders who changed allegiance during the Wars Between the Courts, eventually siding with the Ashikaga in 1364 and receiving from them the provinces of Nagato and Iwami. His son, Yoshihiro (1355–1400), fought for the third Ashikaga Shogun, Yoshimitsu, builder of the Golden Pavilion, and was Yoshimitsu's chief negotiator in the talks which led to the settlement of the claims of the rival dynasties. Several years later he backed the wrong horse by supporting a rival Shogun and perished in battle, leaving his domains to his 5-year-old son. The child thrived under the protection of a benevolent uncle and, on achieving maturity, became one of the avengers of the murdered Shogun Yoshinori, which enhanced the family's reputation. He died without issue and the succession passed eventually to his nephew's grandson, Yoshioki (1477–1528), under whom the clan reached the height of its powers. Yoshioki's greatest achievement was restoring the deposed Shogun Ashikaga Yoshitane to his rightful place,

The 'Parable of the Arrows'. Mori Motonari, avenger of Ouchi and eventual inheritor of his domains, had three sons. As a lesson to them he invited each one to break an arrow, and then demonstrated how difficult it was to break three arrows held together. 'So it must be with you', he added, and the three branch families of Mori, Kobayakawa and Kikkawa showed great loyalty to each other for many decades. Admirers of the Japanese cinema will note that Kurosawa includes an incident similar to this in his film *Ran*.

causing the powerful Hosokawa Sumimoto, whose father had deposed him, to flee before the Ouchi's advance.

Yet, as in so many other cases, the son of this valiant father neglected his military responsibilities and Ouchi Yoshitaka (1507–1551) indulged too freely and unwisely in literature, art and pleasure. Eventually, hearing of the treacherous designs of one of his retainers, Sue Harukata, he called his samurai to arms, only to find that his appeal was ignored by most of them. He then left his castle, where he felt too unsafe, and retired to the temple of Hosen-ji. This too he soon left and fled towards Nagato, where he landed and sought refuge. Here the wretched man was besieged by Sue Harukata and committed suicide. When his son followed suit, 900 years of the Ouchi came to an end.

The rider to the story of Ouchi's downfall is that Sue Harukata did not live long to enjoy his success, but was himself vanquished by another former vassal of the Ouchi, Mori Motonari, at the Battle of Itsukushima (Miyajima) in 1555. Mori Motonari enticed Sue Harukata into making a base on the island, where the Mori destroyed him by a surprise attack. The Mori, having avenged their late masters the Ouchi, went on to become one of the leading *daimyo* in Japan. Such was the nature of *gekokujo*.

The Warlords of the Kanto

As the Ouchi were giving way to the Mori at one end of Honshu, a fierce struggle was continuing 600 miles to the East, in a four-cornered fight for power between the clans of Uesugi, Takeda, Hojo and Imagawa. To a large extent all four represent a more developed form of *daimyo* control than that illustrated by the ancient Ouchi. Of the four mentioned above, only the Imagawa had anything like an illustrious pedigree. The Takeda and the Uesugi were classic examples of post-Onin *gekokujo*. The rise to power of Takeda Shingen (1521–1573), one of the most colourful characters in Japanese history, came about when the youthful Harunobu, as he was known until shaving his head in 1551, discovered that his father planned to disinherit him in favour of a younger brother. Harunobu revolted against his father and placed him in the custody of his father-in-law Imagawa Yoshimoto. Shingen took over the Takeda domain completely, which he ruled efficiently and well. He was one of the few *daimyo* who managed a workable compromise between the need to maintain a large army of reasonably trained troops under experienced samurai, without denuding the rice-fields of agricultural workers. He soon began to expand his territory, largely at the expense of his neighbour, Uesugi Kenshin (1530–1578), with whom he had several military contests where their lands met at at a place called Kawanakajima. There were five 'Battles of Kawanakajima' between 1553 and 1564.

Kenshin, incidentally, in true Sengoku style, was nothing to do with the original Uesugi clan. The Uesugi were an ancient family located around the

The great general Takeda Shingen (1521–1573), as represented by this modern statue in his capital of Kofu. He wears the Buddhist *kesa* over his armour, and a long-sleeved *haori* jacket. His helmet is set off with a horse-hair plume.

site of present-day Tokyo. The clan was, however, almost wiped out by the fourth name mentioned above, the Hojo, who, it must be noted, had nothing to do with the original Hojo! The reason for this confusing scenario is that it was quite common for samurai to change their names, but only the *daimyo* of the Sengoku Period seemed to have appropriated other samurai's names because they sounded better! Both Hojo Soun (1432–1519) and Uesugi Kenshin gave themselves new family names which they felt would improve their social positions. In the case of Hojo Soun (formerly Ise Shinkuro), he married his son to a descendant of the former Hojo *shikken*, who in the past had controlled Shoguns, so as a family name it looked auspicious. As for Kenshin, in 1551 the last of the old Uesugi, Uesugi Norimasa, took refuge with his former vassal after his defeat by the Hojo. The samurai accepted his old master on condition that Uesugi would adopt him as his son and give him the title of Lord of Echigo Province. Norimasa had little choice but to agree and the great *daimyo* Uesugi Kenshin was 'born'.

Changing names was only one of several devices by which a *daimyo* of the Sengoku-jidai could consolidate a position which his sword had won

The tombs of Takeda Shingen and his wife, at the Erin-ji, Enzan, Yamanashi Prefecture.

for him. Other ways were the giving and receiving of hostages and the use of adoption and marriage. We have mentioned hostages before. They were often young children given to an ally as an expression of trust, or demanded from a newly conquered *daimyo* as a guarantee of good behaviour. So blatantly political were adoptive and marriage alliances that they can often be regarded as no more than an extension of the hostage system. No stranger example of adoption exists than that furnished by the Takeda, Hojo and Uesugi. The seventh son of Hojo Ujiyasu (1515–1570), Ujihide, was sent at the age of 10 to be adopted by Takeda Shingen, and, as Takeda Saburo, symbolised and confirmed the alliance between the two clans. When the alliance folded, the Takeda had no further use for him, so he was returned to the Hojo. The Hojo were at that time courting support from the Uesugi, so the young man was sent in turn to Uesugi Kenshin, who adopted him in 1569 as Uesugi Kagetora, the great hope of the Hojo/Uesugi alliance. All went well for Kagetora until Kenshin's death in 1578. It had been Kenshin's wish that his domain be divided equally between Kagetora and his nephew Kagekatsu, but Kagekatsu was greedy and hounded the wretched Kagetora until he committed suicide in 1579.

Marriage was an equally cruel weapon and, among the families of Imagawa, Takeda and Hojo, we may note that Shingen's son, Takeda

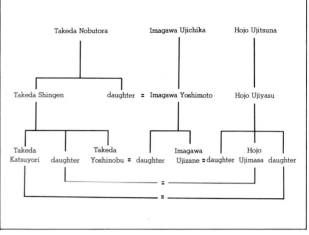

```
Takeda Nobutora        Imagawa Ujichika        Hojo Ujitsuna
       |                       |                      |
   ┌───┴───┐                   |                      |
Takeda Shingen   daughter = Imagawa Yoshimoto    Hojo Ujiyasu
       |                       |                      |
 ┌─────┼──────┐           ┌────┴─────┐          ┌─────┴──────┐
Takeda     Takeda      Imagawa          Hojo
Katsuyori daughter Yoshinobu = daughter Ujizane = daughter Ujimasa daughter
```

Family tree of the Takeda, Imagawa and Hojo families
Marriage was much used in the days of the samurai as a way of cementing military alliances. This diagram shows the remarkably complex relationships that existed between the three families of Takeda, Imagawa and Hojo.

A *ninja* drops from the ceiling on to his victim. This wax dummy hangs menacingly from the ceiling in the Ninja Museum at Iga-Ueno.

Yoshinobu (who was later forced to commit suicide for opposing his father), married Imagawa Yoshimoto's daughter. Imagawa Yoshimoto was himself married to Shingen's sister, who produced the Imagawa heir, Ujizane, who married a daughter of Hojo Ujiyasu. Another daughter of Ujiyasu married Takeda Katsuyori, Shingen's heir, while his son Ujimasa married Shingen's daughter (see above for a diagram of this incredibly complicated system). Uesugi Kenshin, who seems to have kept his vows of celibacy far more rigidly than Shingen, does not seem to have gone in for the marriage market as a means of advancement. There is a strange tradition about Kenshin that 'he' in fact was a woman, but there is no real evidence for such a bizarre twist to the history of the competing *daimyo*. Even stranger are the legends concerned with Kenshin's death, which is supposed to have come about as the result of a totally unexpected swordthrust delivered by a *ninja* who had concealed himself beneath Kenshin's lavatory. The assassin was apparently a dwarf who lived for days among the filth of the closet, waiting for his chance to strike. (The official version was that Kenshin died from an apoplectic fit, which was probably how it looked to attendants who rushed to aid the stricken warlord.)

Of the four warlords here discussed the Hojo were ultimately the most successful, and the longest to last in power. In an age which demanded bigger and better armies a *daimyo's* success began to depend on how skilfully he could turn ignorant tillers of rice-fields into firers of arquebuses and wielders of spears. The Hojo promoted numerous military regulations to this end; the following, on the raising of troops, is a good example:

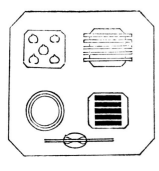

An illustration from the *Gunyoki* depicting the traditional farewell meal taken before battle. It consists of cooked chestnuts, dried *awabi*, *kombu* (seaweed) and *sake* to drink. The whole would be served on a tray to the departing general.

Sashimono must be black and new.

Helmet crests may be either gold or silver. [One assumes that lacquer, and not actual precious metal, is intended.]

The shaft of the pike [spear] must be covered in leather.

Children are not to be brought to camp.

Shields are to be two and a half feet long, one foot wide, and half an inch thick. [This must refer to the wooden shields planted in the ground as a protection for the arquebus troops, though they sound unusually narrow.]

Armour is not to be rolled up. It is to be placed in an armour box. The haori *[jacket] should also be cared for and ready for use.*

Mounted warriors should ride a horse worth one-third of your grant. Although having a horse is troublesome, you must not starve it.

As for your equipment, take care so that it will not be damaged by the elements. The haori *should be made of black cotton. Torn flags and rusty pikes are strictly forbidden.*

It was men such as those to whom the above orders were addressed that helped keep the Hojo supreme in the Kanto until their surrender to Hideyoshi's huge army in 1590.

How different was the fate of the Imagawa! They were ancient and aristocratic, and ruled their domain from their provincial capital of Sumpu (now Shizuoka city) as if it were a miniature version of Kyoto, where they held poetry contests, flower ceremonies and moon-viewing parties. They

PLATE 16 *Oda Nobunaga watches his army march past in 1570*

This plate depicts Oda Nobunaga (1534-1582) watching his army march back to Kyoto after the Battle of the Anegawa in 1570, where he defeated the Asai and Asakura clans. Nobunaga is the pivotal figure in the samurai history of the sixteenth century. Although a very minor *daimyo* compared to the Takeda or the Uesugi it was he who seized the initiative with his victory of Okehazama in 1560. It is also more than likely that it is to Nobunaga that we must look for the impetus in changing the organisation of a samurai army from being a collection of small units under separate, but loyal, commanders, to being a homogeneous force under one commander, divided by function, such as swordsmen, arquebusiers etc, rather than allegiance to clan vassals.

The two samurai on the left wear *sashimono* bearing the Oda *mon*. This *mon*, in black on yellow, was also worn by Nobunaga's *Go-Umawari-shu*, his personal bodyguard. The second samurai has a *sashimono* with another Oda *mon*, a design of Japanese coins. The *ashigaru* behind wear typical smart *okegawa-do*, and support their long *nobori* banners in leather pouches fastened at the waist. The *nobori* were a universal feature of the armies of the time, and tended to indicate units of an army, in contrast to the *uma-jirushi*, the standard, which is illustrated in Plate 24, and is associated with the person of the commander.

Nobunaga is wearing a suit of armour of rather 'old-fashioned' design, but of an elaboration in keeping with his status, and even full *yoroi* armours are found being worn by sixteenth-century commanders. It has *kebiki-odoshi* (close-spaced lacing) of blue silk and is a *do-maru*. The *haidate* are unusual as they consist of numerous metal hexagons sewn on to a cloth backing. His sword is carried *tachi*-style, and he has his *mon* as a *maedate* on his helmet. The armour is preserved in Kyoto, and a photograph of it appears in *The Book of the Samurai* by the present author.

Note the respectful attitude of the common people unlucky enough to have been caught out of doors as the procession marches by!

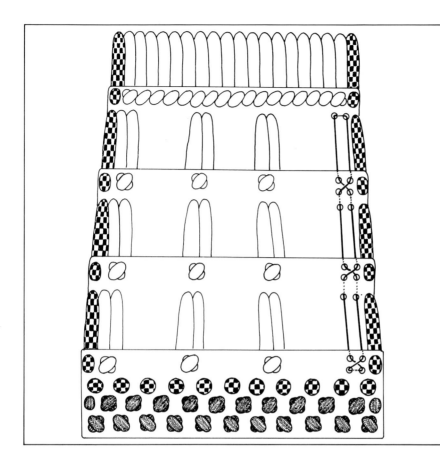

Sugake-odoshi lacing – detail
Sugake (spaced lacing) was introduced during the Muromachi Period. This diagram shows how the spacing was arranged, and illustrates the separate lacing on the bottom plate, which was usually red, regardless of the colour of the rest of the lacing.

were equally skilled in war and situated in much more favourable territory than the mountains of Kenshin and Shingen. Their provinces were flat, rich and bordered the Pacific Ocean, which gave them good lines of communication. In 1560 Imagawa Yoshimoto attempted to do what none of the others had dared – to march on Kyoto and set himself up with a puppet Shogun. He advanced Westward with a huge army, but as the host crossed Owari Province they were observed by one of the upstart *daimyo* that great families like the Imagawa so thoroughly despised. His name was Oda Nobunaga, son of a former peasant warrior whose small territory had been squeezed for a decade between the arms of the Imagawa and their rivals. The Imagawa army, after a modest victory against one of Nobunaga's frontier castles, had rested in a narrow gorge called Okehazama and, under the cover of a fortuitous thunderstorm, the young Oda Nobunaga, outnumbered by twelve to one, attacked their encampment. So speedily did he advance that at first Imagawa Yoshimoto thought a brawl had broken out among his own men. As he rose bareheaded and unprotected from his camp stool he saw a samurai advancing upon him with a drawn sword, and there was no one to save him. The whole Battle of Okehazama took 15 minutes. It finished one clan forever, and threw another onto the forefront of the stage. A new force was abroad – the samurai of Oda Nobunaga.

5

Momoyama Period – Oda Nobunaga

With the rise of Oda Nobunaga we enter the most exciting phase of samurai history. Strictly speaking we are still in the Muromachi Period, because the nominal seat of power remained at Muromachi until Nobunaga abolished the Ashikaga Shogunate in 1573, and the succeeding 'Azuchi-Momoyama' Period dates from Nobunaga's building of Azuchi castle in 1576. We are also quite definitely still in the 'Age of War'! Nevertheless, something happened in 1560 in that obscure little valley called Okehazama that was to change forever the political map of Japan and paved the way for a revolution in samurai warfare. Prior to Nobunaga, the aims of the *daimyo* were limited in scope but, from the time of his defeat of Imagawa, this young warlord acquired a vision of national conquest. Perhaps he was lucky being in the right place at the right time, but it is undoubtedly true that he, alone of all the *daimyo* at the time, knew what to do with such an opportunity when it presented itself.

The Rise of Nobunaga

The victory of Okehazama established Oda Nobunaga as a warrior of the first rank. As well as his undoubted military skills he also had the advantage that geography was on his side, because his province of Owari was set squarely in the fertile lowlands of the Nobi plain, near the present-day city of Nagoya. This also meant that he was quite near to Kyoto, should the opportunity ever arise of emulating Imagawa Yoshimoto's attempts to move on to the capital.

But Nobunaga was not only an accomplished new general, he was also as astute as any of his contemporaries about the need to seek and secure alliances. His victory of Okehazama impressed many, and one of the late Imagawa's generals, who had almost shared in the debacle of Okehazama, was among the first to make a pact with him. This was the famous Tokugawa Ieyasu, Lord of Mikawa, whose family were destined to rise to heights to which the humbly born Nobunaga could not aspire. Nobunaga was also a great believer in political marriages. He was himself married to the daughter of Saito Dosan, once an oil merchant and now the *daimyo* of Mino province, which was the next province between Nobunaga and the

Oda Nobutada, son of Oda Nobunaga, at the Battle of Nagashino 1575.
Oda Nobutada is identified by his *uma-jirushi* banner of a white rectangle within a gold border. This scene is from a modern copy of a well-known painted screen depicting the battle, painted originally for the Kuroda family.

PLATE 17   *A samurai of the Hojo clan rushes to his post in 1574*

Racing full tilt round the walls of Odawara castle comes a samurai of the 'yellow regiment', one of the élite units of the army of the Odawara Hojo. The commander of the 'yellow regiment' was Hojo Tsunanari, the son of an Imagawa retainer called Kushima, who was adopted into the Hojo family. Adoption, and marriage alliances, were very common in the Sengoku Period.

Details of these 'colour regiments' are taken from *Sengoku daimyo* by Sugiyama Hiroshi, who states that the other regiments wore red *sashimono* (under Hojo Tsunataka), blue (Tominaga), white (Kasawara – recruited from Izu Province) and black (Tame). These five commanders were called the five *karo*, or chief retainers. I have assumed that all the *sashimono* would also have borne the Hojo *mon* of a fish-scale design, which is supported by the presence in the Kanagawa Prefectural Art Museum in Yokohama of a red *sashimono* bearing a Hojo *mon* in white.

Our samurai is wearing a *go-mai mogami-do*, which is of solid horizontal plate construction with flanged upper edges, the sections being laced together with *sugake-odoshi*. There are four vertical hinges, giving the whole *do* the appearance of a rounded box. (For an 'exploded-view' see page 82, and for the *sashimono* holder see Plate 27.) The pouch at the front is an addition often found with this style of armour. It is made of blue cloth and fastens with a toggle. The helmet is a *suji-kabuto*, i.e. it has a ridged bowl, and is attractively finished, like the armour, in brown lacquer set off with gold. The gilded *maedate* badge bears the Hojo *mon*. Note the *kohire*, the padded shoulder-supports under the braces of the armour, the neat *ko-sode* (small-plates typical of the period). Note also the fully-developed *mempo* compared with the rudimentary *hoate* face mask in Plate 14. The mask bears snarling features and a bristly horse-hair moustache. A plate, the *yodarekake*, which is suspended from the *mempo*, provides protection for the throat instead of a separate *nodowa*. His *katana* sword is thrust through his belt as it would be if he were not wearing armour, which is possible in a suit of armour, but means the samurai has to hold it in a comfortable position as he runs.

The *haidate* have now evolved into a standard form of chain mail and plates on cloth that was to become practically universal. They are tied behind the thighs. The *suneate*, with a leather pad where the legs touch the stirrup-carriers, will also be seen again. This figure also gives us a clear view of the *waraji*, or straw sandals. There were several ways of tying *waraji*, which were regarded as disposable items.

All in all, apart from various models for the *do*, many of which are illustrated in the following pages, this figure gives us an excellent example of the classic samurai 'battledress' of the late sixteenth century. It is based on several specimens in private collections and a drawing by Sasama.

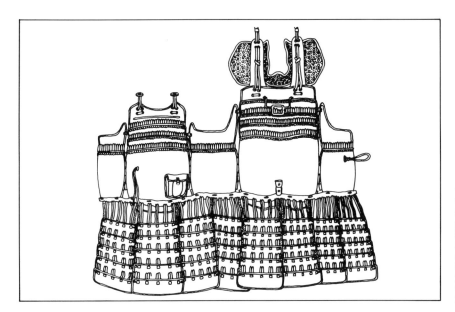

The *mogami-do*
This illustration shows clearly the five-part construction of a typical *go-mai-mogami-do*, such as is illustrated in Plate 17. Various details found on other styles of sixteenth-century armour are also shown here, such as the *kohire*, the padded shoulder-protectors under the shoulder-straps of the armour and the attachments for a *sashimono*.

capital. Beyond Mino was Omi, ruled by Asai Nagamasa, so in the hope of securing his support or neutrality Nobunaga sent his younger sister O-ichi to be Nagamasa's wife. Finally, to protect his rear, Nobunaga promised his daughter in marriage to Takeda Shingen's son. This particular arrangement sealed forever the fate of the Imagawa house, for the threat of Takeda, Oda and Tokugawa being arraigned against him proved too much for Imagawa's heir, Ujizane. He abandoned all attempts at continuing his late father's struggle and sought refuge with his father-in-law, Hojo Ujiyasu, in Odawara castle.

Mino province was the next territory to fall to Nobunaga. In 1556 Saito Dosan was murdered by his son, Nobunaga's brother-in-law, which gave Nobunaga the perfect excuse for invading, on the grounds that he was avenging Dosan's death. He entrusted the campaign to one of the most able of his junior officers, Kinoshita Tokichiro, soon to be known as Toyotomi Hideyoshi, and who with Nobunaga and Tokugawa Ieyasu makes up the trio of the unifiers of Japan. Hideyoshi was a great strategist and showed his talent for assessing topographical features in the siege of Saito's fortress of Inabayama in 1564. Inabayama was built on top of a rocky hill and regarded as impregnable. Indeed, an attack upon it was logically impossible without a similar fortress nearby to act as a base and a refuge. Hideyoshi solved the problem very neatly by constructing the required fortress at Sunomata, under the very gaze of the defenders of Inabayama. His Oda colleagues considered his actions to be foolhardy, but Hideyoshi shamed them all by completing the castle with the help of a local robber chieftain and using it for a swift and successful assault on Inabayama. This placed Mino under Nobunaga's control and gave Hideyoshi a military reputation almost as great as his master's. Nobunaga transferred his capital from Kiyosu to Inabayama, which he re-named Gifu. It was an auspicious name,

Contrary to the popular image of the later Ashikaga Shoguns as idle, effeminate aesthetes, Ashikaga Yoshiteru put up a stout resistance to the attack on him by Miyoshi in 1565, then retired and committed *hara-kiri*.

as Gifu had been the place from which a Chinese warlord had begun his own campaign to unify a kingdom, and the allusion was not lost on Nobunaga's contemporaries. To make his intentions even clearer it was at this time that Nobunaga began using a seal which bore the motto *tenka fubu*, 'the realm covered in military glory'. If further recognition were needed it came the same year in the form of a letter from the Emperor Ogimachi, which began with a reference to Nobunaga as:

Famous general with no equal in any time, most superior in valour, and inspired by the Way of Heaven, since the provinces are now subject to your will it is certain that you will increasingly gain in victories.

The letter goes on to discuss such mundane details as the possibility of Oda Nobunaga repairing the Imperial Palace. Nobunaga, however, could not accept from any Emperor the supreme office of Shogun. For his dream of conquering the Empire to come true he would have to copy the technique of the Hojo *shikken* and rule through somebody else. All Nobunaga needed was a suitable puppet and an excuse to march on Kyoto, and in 1568 the perfect excuse arrived on his doorstep – Ashikaga Yoshiaki, the rightful Shogun.

This Yoshiaki had been a fugitive since the murder of his brother, the Shogun Ashikaga Yoshiteru, in 1565. The attack on Yoshiteru seems to have been every bit as savage and unexpected as the murder of the Shogun Yoshinori in 1441. Once again the conspirators were men close to their victim. One of them, Miyoshi Yoshitsugu, was in fact the commander of the Shogun's own army, which allowed him and his samurai to approach his victim without arousing much suspicion. The Shogun, we are told, fought bravely to the last and committed an honourable act of *hara-kiri*, a fact which contrasts nicely with the traditional view of sixteenth-century Shoguns as impotent, flower-viewing aesthetes. His young cousin Yoshihide, then living as a monk, was dragged from his cloisters and set up as the fourteenth Ashikaga Shogun, to rule in the name of the Miyoshi.

The true heir, Yoshiaki, who escaped, spent several years looking for a *daimyo* who was willing and able to support his cause. His first contact, Rokkaku Yoshisuke, was officially an ally of the Miyoshi and did not dare offend them. His second try, Takeda Shingen, fed him on hope for more than a year, then finally told him he was powerless to act on his behalf. Asakura Yoshikage, *daimyo* of Echizen, who had defeated an army of the Ikko-ikki in 1562 and was Nobunaga's main threat to the North of Kyoto, also refused to help Yoshiaki. Only Nobunaga himself would take the risk. Hideyoshi is supposed to have commented at the time that 'Nobunaga could do nothing without a name', and it was in the name of the Shogun Yoshiaki that Nobunaga began to conquer the Empire.

Nobunaga's first move was to secure his flanks by defeating Rokkaku Yoshisuke in Omi, who fled to Koya-san – a common enough refuge. He then turned his attentions towards the forces of Miyoshi and Matsunaga, whom his army met at the Battle of Sakai. This latter encounter is interesting in that it was described in great detail by one of the first European Jesuit missionaries to Japan, who was an eye-witness to the fighting and had the bizarre honour of celebrating Mass for Christian samurai from both armies during the period of truce prior to the battle. Nobunaga himself was not present, the victory being gained on his behalf by another of his able generals, Shibata Katsuie (1530–1583). The Jesuit account shows a keen appreciation of the political background to it:

After the truce had expired, the two armies marched out of the camps, and drew up in line of battle. Yoshitsugu commanded the right, and Hisahide the left. Both of

---

PLATE 18   *Arquebusiers in action at the Battle of Nagashino, 1575*

Nothing so well illustrates the trust Nobunaga was able to place in his well-disciplined *ashigaru* as his classic victory of Nagashino in 1575. For the Takeda clan it was a disaster. Three years before they had crushed Ieyasu's troops at Mikata-ga-hara with a well-timed cavalry charge, but by 1575 the great Shingen was dead, and it was his brave but foolhardy son, Katsuyori, who hoped to do the same at Nagashino. They charged out of the sun into the eyes, and the muzzles, of 3,000 men of the *teppo-shu*, or arquebus corps. It may be that the slow-loading *teppo* did not mow down hundreds of mounted samurai as is suggested by the popular accounts of Nagashino, but they certainly made an enormous contribution to the victory, if only by destroying the impact of the Takeda samurai advance and thus laying them open to the waiting blades of the swordsmen.

The *teppo-ashigaru* wear simple *okegawa-do* and iron *jingasa* helmets. From their belts hang bullet bags and powder flasks, and round their shoulders are slung ration bags. A coil of fuse is carried round the left arm, and the smouldering match end was not inserted into the serpentine until the last moment. The firing positions of the arquebusiers are taken from contemporary illustrations, which are supported by observations of arquebuses being fired by muzzle-loading enthusiasts in Japan who keep alive the traditions of the *teppo*.

The golden fan standard in the background indicates the presence of Nobunaga's ally, Tokugawa Ieyasu.

them marched through the ranks exhorting their men to signalise themselves this day, on which depended an Empire. They represented to them that Shibata had only a handful of raw and inexperienced men, that Nobunaga, having the Shogun in his power, made this only a sconce for his ambition . . . that being a most bloody and ambitious tyrant, no quarter was to be expected, and so they must either conquer or die.

Shibata, being a great captain, drew up his army into two lines and animated his men to revenge the death of their master [i.e. Ashikaga Yoshiteru] the best of Princes, whom these two barbarous and unnatural rebels had assassinated. . . .

Shibata, seeing his men resolute and determined, marched straight against the enemy, who was also well advanced to receive him. The shock was very rude and bloody, and the victory for a long time seemed doubtful, for the two rebels, seeing life and death depended on the action, played the parts of great captains and soldiers. Shibata, on his part, flew on every side to give necessary orders, and though his army in number proved far inferior to the enemy, yet they far surpassed them in valour and courage.

The victory being very dubious for some time, and Shibata's men beginning to give way, he marched up with a body of reserves, and fell upon Yoshitsugu's right wing with such resolution that he broke through the cavalry and put the infantry in an absolute rout. . . .

The two rebels, seeing their own men upon the flight, followed sword in hand and forced them to wheel about. The cavalry also rallied again, returned to the charge, and the combat was immediately revived. Shame and confusion for the late disgrace spurred on the rebels to repair their honour. The others, on the contrary, puffed up with the late success, looked upon them as already conquered. In effect, after a slight skirmish they took to their heels, and the vanguard, falling upon the rear, put all to confusion. It was then nothing else but a downright butchery and slaughter; and as Shibata aimed principally at the two rebel commanders, he followed close, and charged in the rear; but they, by the help of good horses, saved themselves in the woods and thence retreated into their forts.

Most of the troops cried out for quarter, and went over to Shibata, the rest were all put to the sword.

The war-fan of Takeda Shingen
Commanders of armies customarily carried fans as a means of signalling to troops. This is the rigid version, which is very similar to the ones used nowadays by the referees in sumo wrestling contests. This example was used by Takeda Shingen, and is preserved in the Takeda Museum at the Erin-ji at Enzan, (Yamanashi Prefecture). It is black, with a gold *bonji* on a red disc.

This vivid account paints a dramatic picture of sixteenth-century samurai warfare. Note the control both commanders seem to possess over their samurai until the closing stages and the willingness of some of the Miyoshi/Matsunaga troops to declare for Shibata when they see the cause is hopeless. Suicide was never an automatic choice in samurai warfare.

In the late autumn of 1568 Nobunaga entered Kyoto accompanied by Ashikaga Yoshiaki, who was proclaimed Shogun within the month. Miyoshi and Matsunaga fled before his advance.

The Battle of the Anegawa

In May 1570 Nobunaga moved against the Asakura clan, who threatened

The samurai of the Hojo charge into action
This illustration, from an eighteenth century woodblock printed version of the *Hojo Godaiki*, the "Chronicle of the Five Generations of the Hojo Clan", depicts a charge by samurai of the Hojo. The warrior in the foreground bears the Hojo *mon* of the fish-scale design.

him from the North. As noted above, Asakura Yoshikage was a formidable foe, having scored a notable victory over the Ikko-ikki in 1562, forcing them to be content with the province of Kaga as their domain, and sealing the agreement by giving his daughter in marriage to the Chief Priest of the sect. Nobunaga took the field with 30,000 men, including an army under Tokugawa Ieyasu, and captured two of Asakura's forts, Tezutsu-yama and Kamigasaki, to the North of Lake Biwa. He was about to lay siege to the Asakura fortress of Ichijo-ga-tani when he heard that Asai Nagamasa, Nobunaga's brother-in-law, had allied himself with the Asakura against him. This was a bitter disappointment, for Nobunaga had been relying on this alliance to guard his rear. At a council of his allies both Ieyasu and Matsunaga Hisahide (who had now joined Nobunaga) advised retreat, which they thought would be safe if executed immediately and at speed, for they did not rate Asai's capacity very highly. So Nobunaga started off with the vanguard. Fortunately Matsunaga had a friend who owned the castle of Kuchiki in Omi and went to him to ask for a guide to the by-roads that ran through the mountains to Kyoto via Ohara. Matsunaga went fully prepared to kill him if he refused, but he consented, and Nobunaga was able to lead his men safely back to the capital away from the main roads. Ieyasu and Hideyoshi formed his rearguard, which was harassed all the way and responded on several occasions by vigorous charges against Asakura's men.

Retreats, even when fought bravely and undertaken wisely, are not the most glamorous side of samurai warfare, but Ieyasu and Hideyoshi acquitted themselves well, and the retreat was accomplished with few losses, proving once again that samurai lives were precious and that there was no disgrace in choosing one's own time and place for a reckoning.

It was not long before Nobunaga issued from the capital once again against the Asai and Asakura. This time he advanced from Gifu up the Eastern side of Lake Biwa towards Asai's fortress of Odani, which he menaced by attacking Yokoyama castle on the left bank of the Anegawa to the South-East. This action forced Asai and Asakura into a pitched battle fought across this shallow river, the Battle of the Anegawa (1570). It resulted in a fine victory for Nobunaga with a toll of 3,170 heads, a large proportion of which were taken by the Tokugawa force.

The victory of the Anegawa, though not fully decisive, greatly relieved the pressure on Nobunaga from this quarter. It also meant that he could concentrate on the defeat of his greatest enemy – the adherents and allies

---

PLATE 19 *Warriors of the Ikko-ikki face Nobunaga in 1578*

There is much less material available about the appearance of the fanatical Ikko-ikki than the samurai who opposed them for 50 years. This plate is an attempt to reconstruct the 'feel', if not the actual appearance, of these staunch warriors. The main figure, who shows admirable disregard for the presence of an arrow through his arm, carries his long straight spear as he advances across the swampy ground of the Nagashima River delta towards Nobunaga's troops, to whom the Ikko-ikki were as contemptible as vermin. We have given him a very simple *hara-ate* of metal plates on cloth, and a white *hachimaki* headband strengthened with chain mail. His shaven head is growing hair again.

His fallen comrade in the foreground wears a folding version of samurai armour, which we know was worn by the defenders of the fortress-cathedral of Ishiyama Hongan-ji, and the stockades of Nagashima. He wears a *sashimono* that has been preserved, which bears the crudely-written slogan, 'He who advances is sure of heaven, but he who retreats will suffer hell.' Thousands of these flags must have existed. The other white flag bears a Buddhist slogan beginning 'Namu...' ('Hail to...'). The red flag with the *sotoba* design was carried by a contingent from the Zempuku-ji of Edo who supported the Ishiyama Hongan-ji against Nobunaga's attempts to destroy it.

The Nagashima area is still wild and mysterious to this day, in spite of being crossed by a railway line and several bridges over the reed swamps, and in misty weather one can easily conjure up images of the thousands of Ikko fanatics who were slaughtered here by Oda Nobunaga.

of the Ikko-ikki. The Ikko-ikki were the hub around which rolled a wheel of ever-changing alliances against Nobunaga, and a major part of his career was taken up by opposing this political focus that drew all opposition to Nobunaga into itself.

Nobunaga and the Ikko-ikki

The Ikko-ikki had continued to grow into the 1570s. Not only were the Ikko-ikki a powerful military force, they also had the ability to embarrass Nobunaga's *tenka* by various economic weapons, such as the withholding of taxes and rents. Their temples, also, existed ostentatiously as independent towns. What was of fundamental importance to Nobunaga was that the power of the Ikko-ikki was concentrated at the very places where *he* had to be powerful. There were Ikko strongholds in his native Province of Owari, in his early conquest, Mino, in the 'Home Provinces' that guarded Kyoto and in the strategic areas of Kaga and Echizen – all were vital to both interests, and there could be no compromise.

In his letters and despatches Nobunaga reserves his strongest language for the Ikko-ikki. They must be 'wiped out', 'eradicated', 'mown down'. No samurai honour was involved with this enemy. They would be searched out and destroyed *yama yama, tani tani*, 'on every hill and valley', as he wrote to the Governor of Kyoto in 1575, after massacring 20,000 of the sect's adherents in Echizen.

The religious nature of the Ikko-ikki attracted support from the older established organisations of militant clergy. In 1570 the Ishiyama Hongan-ji, the Ikko's fortified cathedral in Osaka, sent help to the Miyoshi faction, which was again stirring up trouble in Kyoto, and which was joined by *sohei* from Negoro in Kii Province, who included 3,000 arquebusiers in their ranks. Almost at the same time Asai and Asakura made an alliance with the veteran soldier monks of the Enryaku-ji on Mount Hiei, and Ikko-ikki from Ise Province threatened Nobunaga from the East. Nobunaga's tactics were reduced to holding the line from Kyoto to Gifu, but he reacted by mounting an attack that was as much symbolic as it was designed to destroy the particular faction of his enemies against whom it was launched – the destruction of Mount Hiei. In both it was successful. The *sohei* of Mount Hiei, who had provided a refuge for rebels and Emperors for centuries, were destroyed forever as a military force as Nobunaga's samurai advanced up the holy mountain, hacking, burning and shooting to death any living thing that opposed them. As a symbol of his determination to crush all manifestations of the warrior monk the campaign send a shudder through the forts of the Ikko-ikki. Here was a warlord who meant every word he had used about them. Only one religious sect applauded. They were the Christian missionaries from Portugal, who saw in Nobunaga a destroyer of the 'enemies of God'.

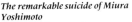

The remarkable suicide of Miura Yoshimoto
The author has noted many unusual acts of suicide in the annals of the samurai, ranging from jumping headlong from a horse with a dagger half way down one's throat to being buried alive, but none are as bizarre as the act credited to a certain Miura Yoshimoto who, during a fierce battle at Arai Castle against the Hojo in 1516, cut off his own head! Japanese swords were renowned for their sharpness, and Yoshimoto used one by the famous Masamune, but it remains open to conjecture as to whether such a deed could be physically possible. It is recorded with much admiration in the *Hojo-Godaiki*, and this illustration is taken from a woodblock printed edition, which has modified the story slightly to show Yoshimoto dismounted when he performs the amazing act.

Nobunaga's campaign against the Ikko-ikki was conducted against a background of a growing estrangement between himself and the Shogun, whose position gave other *daimyo* an excuse to act against Nobunaga. Takeda Shingen in fact inflicted a defeat upon Nobunaga's ally Tokugawa Ieyasu at Mikata-ga-hara in 1572, and only the death of this redoubtable warlord in 1573 reduced the threat from the powerful Takeda war machine.

In 1573 Nobunaga sent Ashikaga Yoshiaki into exile, bringing the sorry history of the Ashikaga Shogunate to its end. The following month Nobunaga turned again towards Omi. As his army approached Asai Nagamasa's Odani castle, the latter appealed to Asakura Yoshikage for support. When Asakura began to lead his army towards his ally, Nobunaga intercepted him and chased the survivors back to Ichijo-ga-tani, where Yoshikage was forced to commit suicide. The Oda army turned back and easily overcame Asai Nagamasa, who also took his own life. Their heads were displayed in public in Kyoto, then lacquered and gilded to preserve for posterity Nobunaga's destruction of two samurai warriors. He awarded their lands to Hideyoshi, who built a castle at Nagahama, on the shores of Lake Biwa.

The time was ripe for Nobunaga to continue his military opposition to the Ikko-ikki. He began by isolating the Ishiyama Hongan-ji from its other satellites. Several times since 1570 he had suffered risings by a branch of the Ikko sect based in a fortress called Nagashima, on the estuary of the Kiso-gawa. In July 1574 Nobunaga attacked Nagashima, helped by a force of pirates from Ise, who bombarded the Ikko-ikki from the seaward side with heavy calibre muskets. By the end of August they were short of food and willing to treat, but Nobunaga was not inclined towards mercy. Instead he built a stockade around the two fortresses that still held out, Nakae and Nagashima itself, into which had crammed as many as 20,000 people. These fortresses were then set on fire, and anyone who attempted to escape through the palisade was shot down.

The Master of Musketry

The following year, 1575, Nobunaga's confidence was greatly increased by his classic victory of the Battle of Nagashino, where the late Takeda Shingen's son and heir Katsuyori was induced to use the legendary Takeda cavalry charge against Nobunaga's army, which had sheltered itself behind a loose palisade. Volley after volley of arquebus balls tore into the advancing Takeda samurai, until, confused and disorganised, they fell prey to the sharp swords of Nobunaga's army.

Nobunaga was by no means the first *daimyo* to use firearms. They had been known in Japan since 1542, when two arquebuses had been demonstrated to the local *daimyo* by some shipwrecked Portuguese sailors.

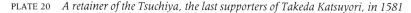

PLATE 20   *A retainer of the Tsuchiya, the last supporters of Takeda Katsuyori, in 1581*

The nemesis for the Takeda clan came in 1581. Takeda Katsuyori, defeated at Nagashino, was gradually abandoned by his father Shingen's old retainers as Oda Nobunaga and Tokugawa Ieyasu advanced into the mountains of Kai. Only the Tsuchiya were with him to the last. Tsuchiya Masatsugu had been one of the 'Takeda Twenty-four Generals' to be killed at Nagashino, and it was three brothers of the succeeding generation who were to die with him at Temmoku-zan.

This proud samurai, with the Tsuchiya *mon* on his *sashimono*, is wearing a *tatami-gusoku* (folding armour) – the simplest samurai armour of all. It consisted of a series of plates sewn on to a cloth backing and joined by links of mail. He has no *haidate*, or *sode*, but good *oda-kote*, the style of sleeve armour that had raised gourd-shaped plates. The *shikoro* of his helmet is made in the same way as his armour, but its bowl is of much stouter construction, being a typical *zunari-*, or *hineno-kabuto*. He is standing on the bridge leading to the entrance of one of Katsuyori's castles. Katsuyori was fond of castles, and many saw in his reliance upon passive defence a bad omen for the Takeda clan. The armour is based upon several extant specimens and drawings by Sasama.

The courtyard of the Honno-ji in Kyoto, the site of the assassination of Oda Nobunaga in 1582.

Two samurai armed with arquebuses. The introduction of firearms was the most decisive development in the whole of samurai warfare. At the Battle of Nagashino in 1575, Oda Nobunaga used hundreds of arquebuses to inflict a major defeat on the Takeda clan cavalry, an engagement commemorated every year on the site of Nagashino castle. The equipment of these two 'samurai' is authentic, with the addition of plastic bags to protect their weapons against the persistent rain that accompanied the 1986 celebrations!

Within months the swordsmiths of Japan, who were already highly skilled in metalwork, were turning out copies of the weapons and improving the design. There is little doubt that Nobunaga acquired a healthy respect for firearms when they were used against him. As early as 1560, during Imagawa's attempted march through his province, Tokugawa Ieyasu had made good use of concentrated arquebus fire in taking Nobunaga's fortress of Marune. The Ikko-ikki had their own large arsenal, and a ball from one of their arquebuses wounded Nobunaga in the leg during one of his attempts to take the Ishiyama Hongan-ji. But Nobunaga's decision to use arquebuses on a large scale, in a field battle, protected by field fortifications, and operating under such good discipline that some rudimentary form of rotational volley firing could take place, has the hallmark of an innovatory military genius.

The Ishiyama Hongan-ji was not quelled so easily. Its position on the watery delta of Osaka enabled the Mori clan to ferry supplies to it along the Inland Sea. In the summer of 1575 Nobunaga fought a sea battle during which many guns were used, in an attempt to prevent these supplies from getting through. The subsequent failure made him return to his original policy of isolating Ishiyama Hongan-ji by reducing its satellite fortresses. In 1577 he destroyed the Ikko strongholds at Saiga and the *sohei* of Negoro in Kii Province, and Ishiyama Hongan-ji stood alone. Only a combined attack on Nobunaga by Mori from the West and Uesugi Kenshin from the East could save it, but by 1578 Uesugi Kenshin was dead (perhaps the *ninja* in his lavatory was sent by Nobunaga?) and Mori, the warlord of the West, dared not move alone. Gradually the Ikko-ikki's resistance faded and in 1580, following the advice of the Emperor, the Ishiyama Hongan-ji, the last outpost of militant Buddhism, surrendered to Nobunaga.

In 1581 Nobunaga put on a splendid military parade through the streets of Kyoto, ostensibly for the pleasure of the Emperor, but in reality to impress upon the population Nobunaga's continuing triumph. It was almost his last flamboyant act. In 1582 Toyotomi Hideyoshi was besieging Takamatsu castle and sent an urgent plea to Nobunaga for reinforcements. Nobunaga responded rapidly, but thereby left himself perilously unguarded, and he was attacked in the Honno-ji temple in Kyoto by another of his generals, Akechi Mitsuhide. Nobunaga's bodyguard were taken by surprise as thoroughly as he had once ambushed Imagawa Yoshimoto. The Honno-ji was burned and, as the temple blazed around him, Nobunaga committed a defiant act of suicide. As word spread that he was dead the avaricious townspeople looted his glorious castle of Azuchi and burned it to the ground.

6

Momoyama Period
– Toyotomi Hideyoshi

The second of the trio whose military conquests unified Japan, and brought to an end the 'warring states' of the *daimyo*, was Toyotomi Hideyoshi (1539–1598), who is often referred to as the 'Napoleon of Japan'.

Toyotomi Hideyoshi

Akechi Mitsuhide, the destroyer of Nobunaga, bears the nickname of the 'Thirteen Day Shogun', which indicates approximately how long he lasted before being defeated by Nobunaga's protegé, Toyotomi Hideyoshi, at the Battle of Yamazaki. Hideyoshi, who managed to contrive for himself the inheritance of Nobunaga's *tenka*, in spite of opposition from practically all of Nobunaga's allies, enemies and surviving relatives, is one of the most fascinating characters in samurai history. He was the son of a woodcutter and joined Nobunaga's army as an *ashigaru*. He rose through the ranks on merit alone. Following Nobunaga's death he was able to turn the squabbles about inheritance and policy to his own considerable advantage, helped along by a number of profitable sieges and battles, such as Shizugatake in

---

PLATE 21 *Tokugawa Ieyasu at the Battle of Nagakute, 1584*

The Battle of Nagakute in 1584 was one of Tokugawa Ieyasu's finest victories. Here we see him in command wearing the actual armour which he is supposed to have worn there. It is preserved in the Kunozan Toshogu Shrine Treasure House in Shizuoka. It is a remarkably simple affair for such an important commander, but as such reflects Ieyasu's eminently practical approach to life.

The armour is a *nuinobe-do*, of solid horizontal plates joined by *sugake-odoshi*. The scalloped top edges are a feature often found on a *nuinobe-do*, whereby it differs from the *mogami-do* shown in Plate 17, which has flanged upper edges. This armour is also of *ni-mai*, two-piece, style, similar to the *okegawa-do*, and again differing from the *go-mai* five-sections, of the Hojo armour. (A *nuinobe-do* laced with cross knots would be called a *hishinui-do*.)

The *kote* are of very dense chain mail, which is far more 'European-looking' than many Japanese examples. His *haidate* and *suneate* are quite ordinary. The helmet is very splendid, being of an almost square cross section, and is set off with a delicate fern-leaf *maedate* crest with a devil's face. There is a second *shikoro*, the *shita-shikoro*, of mail on cloth, and a very fine *mempo* with moustache and beard. Ieyasu is pointing with his *saihai*, which has tassels of oiled paper.

The *maku* curtains bear the Tokugawa *mon*, and the banner of the Ii family can be seen going by behind.

The Battle of Nagakute in 1584 arose out of an attempt by Ikeda Tsuneoki, one of Hideyoshi's generals, to outflank Ieyasu's lines at Komaki and make a rapid raid into Mikawa. Here we see a detachment of Ikeda's arquebus corps negotiating a narrow mountain pass with the help of rope ladders.

1583. At the siege of Kameyama, Hideyoshi achieved the first victory in samurai history by the use of mining. At Shizugatake he surprised his enemy by a rapid advance by night. There seemed no end to his boldness. Though he had the physical appearance, and to some extent the shape, of a wizened monkey, as his contemporaries describe him, he is also admired as 'a veritable war-god on the field of battle'.

Only Tokugawa Ieyasu provided a counter to him at the indecisive Battle of Nagakute in 1584. The two generals had glared at each other from extensive field fortifications near Komaki, which is today a suburb of Nagoya. Defence was not a mode of warfare that appealed to the samurai spirit, so Hideyoshi sent Ikeda on a secret raid into Ieyasu's Mikawa. The Tokugawa observed his army and attacked them near Nagakute. It was a bloody encounter and the unfortunate Ikeda lost his head, but Nagakute served, in the short term at any rate, to gain him a valuable ally, as both recognised the other's obvious merit. There was nothing to be gained from opposing one another. Together they could conquer an Empire.

As Hideyoshi had risen from the peasant class to become a commander of samurai, one of his first steps after achieving national control was to ensure that no one could follow in his footsteps. By his edict of 1587, known as the 'Great Sword Hunt', all non-samurai were forcibly disarmed.

The sword-collectors explained to the enraged populace that the weapons so gathered were to be melted down and made into nails and bolts for the huge statue of Buddha which Hideyoshi was building. Their compliance with the edict would therefore ensure their salvation in the next world, as well as benefiting the peace of the present life.

Hideyoshi the Castle-Builder

Hideyoshi's career becomes more remarkable once Nobunaga's domain has been secured and he is able to look further afield. One of his first steps was to build a mighty castle at Osaka, on the site of the Ishiyama Hongan-ji. Hideyoshi is known as a great castle-builder, and the huge white-walled fortress upon a sloping stone base is almost the symbol of the Momoyama Period, but he was also, like Nobunaga before him, a great destroyer of castles – other people's, of course! His overall plan was to reduce the number of fortresses throughout the country, leaving only the strategic provincial castles of the great *daimyo* whom he had subdued and who had sworn loyalty towards him, thus reducing the risk of rebellion against them or Hideyoshi himself. The castles that arose during the latter part of the sixteenth century were much larger and stronger than the more modest structures that had preceded them, as illustrated by documents referring to the Hojo family. The Hojo were great castle-builders, as evidenced by their central stronghold of Odawara and the various satellite fortresses that protected their domains. Birt's study of the Hojo comments:

Castle repair was a highly organised task in the Sengoku period and an important responsibility of the castellan. It was also highly detailed, as revealed in a 1563

According to tradition, Toyotomi Hideyoshi not only built a fortress at Sunomata to oppose the mighty Inabayama, but built the whole structure in one night to impress his enemies! Here we see Hideyoshi's men furiously engaged on castle-building.

castle repair order to the residents of Tana village for work on Tamanawa castle. The order stated that if there were no typhoons, the walls were to be repaired every five years. The rate of work was set at four persons per ken [6 feet] *per day. The villagers were also ordered to bring the following materials:*

5 large posts	*10 bundles of Yamato bamboo*
5 smaller posts	*30 coils of rope*
10 bamboo poles	*20 bundles of reed*

The villagers were then given precise instructions for raising the palisade. They were ordered to: drive in the large wooden posts at intervals of one ken *in the earthworks; in between these posts, they spread sideways two bamboo sticks, and then arranged four bundles of Yamato bamboo; this was fastened by six coils of rope and then thatched with reed. The walls were eight* sun [10 inches] *thick, and were coated with a mixture of red clay and rock to make them durable. Given these materials and the method of construction, it is easy to see why the Sengoku castle required constant upkeep to maintain a battleworthy condition.*

Wood and earth were the main material for the Sengoku castles, but some stone was used for towers and gateways. It was the ill-fated Azuchi, and the colossal Osaka, which set the new standard for castle-building. Now stone was used for walls and parapets and the whole scale of castle-building became colossal. Nearly all the Japanese castles that remain to this day were completed at this time, though many have been much restored since.

PLATE 22   *Kato Kiyomasa collects a head during the Battle of Sendaigawa in 1587*

The Battle of Sendaigawa, the Sendai River, was the last major encounter fought by Hideyoshi's troops as they battled their way down the island of Kyushu to defeat the powerful Shimazu clan of Satsuma. (There is a full account of the campaign in *The Samurai – a Military History* by the present author.)

Kato Kiyomasa (1562–1611) was one of Toyotomi Hideyoshi's most renowned generals. He was born the son of the village blacksmith in Nakamura, which is now a suburb of Nagoya. Nakamura was also the home village of his mentor, Hideyoshi. At the Battle of Shizugatake in 1583 Kiyomasa was named as one of the *shichi hon yari*, the 'Seven Spears' who fought most valiantly that day.

In this plate we see him in a suit of armour which he is known to have worn, though it is not entirely certain if he wore it during the Kyushu campaign. It is preserved in the Tokyo National Museum in Ueno Park, Tokyo. Its strange design is supposed to represent the body of a monk. The *do* is an extreme version of a smooth-surfaced *hotoke-do*, which has been beaten to represent skin clinging to wasted ribs, and is finished in a most unusual pink lacquer. The left side of the *do* has been laced in *iro-iro odoshi* (multi-coloured lacing) to look like a monk's robe. The *kusazuri* are finished in the same way. The helmet is not Kiyomasa's favourite 'court-cap' style, but one designed to continue the theme of the human body. On the scalp is horse-hair

combed back into a pigtail with a heavy peak.

Kiyomasa's unfortunate victim wears a *dangaie-do*, which is a *nuinobe-do* that has its upper plates laced in *sugake-odoshi* and its lower plates laced in *kebiki-odoshi*. As he has no doubt regarded himself as a person of some importance he has dispensed with a *sashimono*, and replaced the upper bracket for holding a *sashimono* by a small version of the old *agemaki* bow, which now serves no practical purpose.

In the background are samurai wearing the Shimazu *sashimono*, based on one dating from the time of Hideyoshi's adversary, Shimazu Yoshihiro, which is preserved in the museum of Shimazu memorabilia in Kagoshima City.

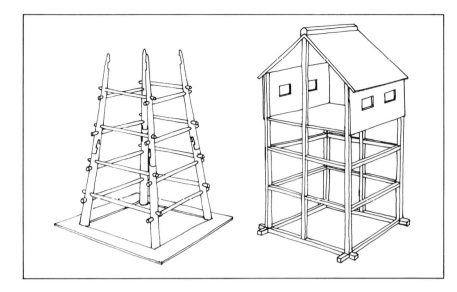

The siege tower
The author has been unable to find any contemporary reference for the use of the type of moveable siege towers familiar from Medieval Europe. Japanese siege towers tend to be immobile contructions designed to afford observation facilities rather than provide an assault platform. Some are of open construction, others solid-looking structures very similar to the permanent towers of the early sixteenth-century wooden castle such as seen in Plate 15.

The castles of Japan may be Hideyoshi's lasting monument, but his intangible legacy was a tradition of military excellence that sent highly-trained, well-equipped armies from one end of Japan to another, as he completed the work Nobunaga had begun. He became the first *daimyo* to overcome the two other main islands of Shikoku and Kyushu. His Kyushu campaign, in particular, was an outstanding achievement, as it involved controlling armies from a distance, forming alliances as well as fighting fierce samurai battles.

The Christian Samurai

Hideyoshi is also remembered for his persecution of the Christians, a trend which reversed Nobunaga's policy towards them. Nobunaga had sheltered the missionaries from Buddhist opposition, but as they rejoiced over the destruction of Mount Hiei, and applauded Nobunaga's quelling of the Ikko sect, little did his Jesuit friends suspect that they were seeing a pattern for the repression of religious movements that would be used against them before the century was out. The Jesuits had served Nobunaga's purposes as a lever against the Buddhist fanatics and a channel of goodwill that permitted the free flow of cannon and gunpowder into his castle storerooms. Hideyoshi soon came to see them in a very different light. Organised religion – any organised religion – posed a threat to loyalty, and that could not be tolerated. But what threat did Christianity pose?

From the point of view of samurai history any direct 'threat' was negligible. Never at any time was there an exclusively Christian army comparable to the fanatics of the Ikko-ikki or the *sohei* of Mount Hiei. *Daimyo* who had embraced Christianity saw to it that their followers received baptism, but although such men may have gone into battle with

A nineteenth-century painting on silk, copied from an original Western-style portrait of the Christian samurai, Takayama Ukon.

crosses on their banners and shouting Christian war-cries, they fought for the *daimyo*'s cause. It is at an individual level that we must look for illustration of the Christian samurai, and the Momoyama Period furnishes several suitable examples. One such was Takayama Ukon. He was born in either 1552 or 1553, and died in 1615, so his life encompasses exactly the time between St Francis Xavier's death, at the height of missionary activity, and Tokugawa Ieyasu's order expelling the missionaries from Japan.

He was baptised at the age of 11 and given the Christian name of Justo, at the same time as his father, Takayama 'Darie'. The Takayama were vassals of the Wada family, and when Wada Koremasa was killed in Nobunaga's service they found themselves under his successor, Wada Korenaga, who was the owner of Takatsuki castle, a fortress placed somewhat uncomfortably between Osaka and Kyoto, and entirely surrounded by the territory of the *daimyo*, Araki Muneshige. Wada Korenaga was jealous of the reputation the Takayama family enjoyed and contrived to have them murdered during a dinner party at his castle. The plot was discovered, and Ukon fought back so successfully that Korenaga fled wounded. Nobunaga, impressed by their reaction, transferred the castle to Ukon, who began to take a full part in his campaigns. We hear of him fighting against the Ishiyama Hongan-ji, but his greatest test came off the field of battle, when his overlord Araki Murashige revolted against Nobunaga in 1578.

Ukon had advised Araki not to side against Nobunaga, but as he was his vassal he was sworn to support him, and had sent his sister and her son as hostages to Araki for good behaviour. Nobunaga, however, realised Ukon's deep Christian commitment, and hoped to use it to persuade the young man into surrendering Takatsuki castle to him. He sent a Jesuit to Ukon, who bore a message from Nobunaga stating that he would execute the

---

PLATE 23   *Kato Kiyomasa's army creates havoc against the Koreans in 1592*

In this plate Kato Kiyomasa is seen engaging the Korean army during the Korean War of 1592–1598. In contrast to Plate 22 he is wearing one of the *naga-eboshi-kabuto* helmets for which he is famous. They were made by building up a false crown of wood and papier-mache on to a basic *zunari-kabuto*. The silver-lacquered one shown here is taken from a replica displayed in the museum of Hideyoshi and Kiyomasa in Nakamura Park, Nagoya, the birthplace of these heroes. The original is in the Tokugawa Art Museum in Nagoya, but is rarely displayed. Two different designs are in the Hommyoji

Museum, Kumamoto, and Kumamoto castle. He wears a red *jinbaori* and a *mogami-do*, with flanged upper edges.

His samurai and *ashigaru* are in 'battle dress' of *okegawa-do*. There is more variety among the samurai, as may be imagined, but the overall uniformity indicates the gradual separation of the warrior from the land that was going on during the Age of War. Soon even the lowliest *ashigaru* would become a samurai, and spend no more time tilling fields. They all wear the Kato *mon* on their *sashimono* and, in some cases, on their armour.

In the background flies

Kiyomasa's *uma-jirushi* standard, a long *hata-jirushi* bearing the motto and war-cry of the Nichiren sect of Buddhism, of which Kiyomasa was a member. It reads *Namu myoho renge kyo* ('Glory to the Holy Lotus'). Nichiren taught that salvation was to be found in the Lotus Sutra, hence these words.

The Korean costumes are based on trophies brought back to Japan after the Korean War, of which there are only a few examples, and on specimens displayed in the Central Historical Museum, P'yong-yang, North Korea, to whose staff the author expresses his gratitude.

Top right of illustration, Japanese text:
鳥　　鯱　城　の
ヱ　　ヲ　中　ス
ノ　　鰍　の
圖

Maeda Toshiie, Lord of Kaga
Maeda Toshiie was one of
Hideyoshi's most successful generals,
and acquired control over much of
the Hokurikudo Region of Japan.
This statue of him is in his capital of
Kanazawa, and behind the statue
may be seen the towers of the
Ishikawa Gate of Kanazawa Castle,
which is all that remains of his
fortress. Toshiie is wearing a gold-
lacquered armour, with a
spectacular gold-lacquered catfish-
tail helmet.

The defenders starve during a siege
Toyotomi Hideyoshi was a master of
siegecraft, and the extremes to
which the defenders could be
reduced is depicted sensationally in
this illustration from *Ehon Taikoki*,
an illustrated life of Hideyoshi, of
which several different versions
exist. In the bottom right a group
share a raw horse's leg, while others
appear to be preparing for
cannibalism.

Shibata Katsuie takes an enemy's head
Shibata Katsuie is best known for being the leader of the army defeated by Hideyoshi at the Battle of Shizugatake in 1583, when his general Sakuma Morimasa disobeyed his orders to remain in a fortified position. Katsuie was an accomplished leader of samurai, and this picture from the *Ehon Taikoki* shows him in happier days when he fought side by side with Hideyoshi in the service of Nobunaga. He is taking an enemy's head in grand style.

missionaries and destroy the churches in his domains unless Ukon handed over the castle. Takayama Ukon was placed in a frightful dilemma. His samurai honour, linked to the lives of his sister and nephew, had been placed as a counterbalance to his Christianity. After hours of agonised prayer he presented himself before Nobunaga as a supplicant, unarmed, and with a symbolically shaved head. Nobunaga was much impressed by Ukon's sincerity. Naturally, he took over the castle, but when the campaign was concluded he pardoned Ukon and increased his domains. Araki Murashige, too, had been impressed by Ukon's behaviour and did not harm any of the hostages.

Later Takayama Ukon took part in the Battle of Yamazaki at which Akechi Mitsuhide, Nobunaga's assassin, was defeated, and then came under the influence of Hideyoshi. At Nobunaga's funeral he declined to offer incense at the Buddhist altar, which may have offended Hideyoshi, but all was forgiven when Ukon took a valiant part in the Battle of Shizugatake in 1583. He was the commander of the frontier fortress of Iwasaki-yama, from which he was driven by an impetuous attack from Sakuma Morimasa. This was the attack that was to prove to be Sakuma's undoing when Hideyoshi brought over his rapid reinforcements. Although wounded in the encounter, and suffering the loss of many retainers, Takayama's defeat was instrumental in Hideyoshi's victory. He therefore gained greatly in standing with Hideyoshi, and went on to join in his expeditions to Shikoku and against the *sohei* of Negoro in Kii.

Those were the good years, but the conflict of loyalty remained and Takayama Ukon was but one of a number of Christian *daimyo* whose loyalty to the growing power of Hideyoshi could not be absolute. For Hideyoshi the key lay in a historical analogy. The Buddhist sect of Jodo-Shinshu, in its social and political manifestation of the Ikko-ikki, had brought great harm to the country until Nobunaga crushed it. Christianity, in his eyes, was no different. Thus began the unhappy times of persecution, which culminated in the martyrdom of the Twenty-Six Saints, who were crucified at Nagasaki on 5 February 1597. Hideyoshi also decreed that all the Christian fathers should leave the country, but his death in 1598 prevented him from carrying out this order.

For the next decade the Christian *daimyo* enjoyed a respite from persecution, until the Tokugawa regime became wary of them for the same reasons as Hideyoshi. Ukon was then living under the protection of Maeda Toshinaga, the *daimyo* of Kanazawa. In 1614 the Tokugawa Shogunate issued a decree expelling all missionaries and ordering the banishment of Takayama Ukon and other *daimyo*. Toshinaga's successor, Toshitsune,

---

PLATE 24   *Toyotomi Hideyoshi urges his troops to the siege of Odawara, 1590*

'In stature he resembled a wizened monkey, but on the field of battle he was a veritable war-god', wrote one contemporary of the 'Napoleon of Japan', Toyotomi Hideyoshi (1536–1598). This plate captures the dynamic presence of the leader who rose from being Nobunaga's sandal-bearer to become commander of tens of thousands. His armies conquered the island clans of Shikoku and Kyushu, gained an almost bloodless victory over the Hojo of Odawara and sent an invasion force to Korea.

It is the defeat of the Hojo that is illustrated here. Hideyoshi is wearing a black-lacquered helmet with a 'sunburst' crest at the rear. The original of this helmet has long since perished, but a faithful copy is on display in Osaka Castle Museum. He is pointing with his *warfan*, a delicate design of pearls on red silk, which still exists. He wears a *jinbaori*, or armour-surcoat, which was *de rigueur* for samurai generals, and was often richly embroidered.

Behind him stands his *uma-jirushi* (literally 'horse insignia') which was the name given to the commander's standard. Ieyasu used a large golden fan (see Plate 18) and Nobunaga had a huge red umbrella. Hideyoshi's was known as the 'golden gourd', the gourd being his original *mon*, and he is traditionally supposed to have added a gourd for every victory he won, until the final version shown here was known as the 'Thousand-gourd standard'. The Toyotomi *mon* of the paulownia is on the dangling black strips in front of the curtain of red tassels.

城中渇に臨ぐ
六角の使者を
欺く

Taking a bath
This illustration, taken from the *Ehon Taiko-ki*, probably depicts a scene during the siege of Chokoji in 1570, where Shibata Katsuie earned much praise. The defending warriors are bathing. The *fundoshi* or loincloth, and the characteristic samurai hairstyle may be clearly noted.

高松の城
水攻
大結構
とて
成得る

The siege of Takamatsu Castle 1582
One of Hideyoshi's greatest achievements was the reduction of the Mori clan's fortress of Takamatsu. Noticing that it lay on low ground, Hideyoshi's engineers diverted a river, and with the help of a series of dykes the whole castle was flooded. It was during this siege that Hideyoshi received word of the murder of Nobunaga.

feared that Ukon would take up arms against him to defend himself against the expulsion order, but Ukon wrote to him saying, 'I do not strive for my salvation with weapons but with patience and humility, in accordance with the doctrine of Jesus Christ.'

On 8 November 1614 he sailed for Manila, together with the other expelled missionaries and native Christians. Forty days later he fell ill and died. He is honoured today in Japan as a man who combined within himself the two virtues of the noble samurai and the staunch Christian.

111

The Fall of the Hojo

By 1590 all of Japan had yielded to Hideyoshi except for the proud Hojo clan, who felt themselves to be safe behind the walls of Odawara and the outer, natural walls of the Hakone Mountains. We have seen earlier how the Hojo organised the repair of their minor castles. The main fortress of Odawara was in a much bigger league, built on the style of Osaka, with much use of stone in its construction. When Hideyoshi's intentions to destroy it became clear, orders went out for all samurai to pull back from the satellite castles into the safety of Odawara, and to bring their wives and children with them, a means of ensuring their safety and also encouraging a full participation in the fighting.

The castle almost burst with soldiers. Contemporary accounts describe how the roads between the duty stations were choked with troops, whose camps were so crowded that they resembled bamboo groves. Nevertheless the Hojo were hopelessly outnumbered. In all their forces cannot have been larger than 50,000 men, while Hideyoshi was able to mobilise as many as 200,000. He attacked the Hojo from three sides and, knowing how strongly defended the castle was, decided to starve them out. A small town grew up outside Odawara's walls, where Hideyoshi's samurai played *go* and grew vegetables. The only really fierce fighting occurred as a result of an attempt at treachery which backfired. A certain Natsuda Norihide, who was in charge of one of the gates, offered to betray the castle to Hideyoshi in return for a reward. His plot was discovered, and his troops replaced by reliable fighters, so that when Hideyoshi's men attacked they were met by a fierce resistance. Like other raids, however, it served to alleviate the boredom of the long siege. With the fall of Odawara the last of the independent *daimyo*, whose success had been a model for others, committed suicide. Their territory was given to Tokugawa Ieyasu, who established his headquarters not at Odawara but at the castle in a little fishing village nearby called Edo. It was a successful foundation, for this village of Edo is now the city of Tokyo.

PLATE 25 *Kuroda Nagamasa, bringing reinforcements to Korea in 1592, is attacked by the turtle ships.*

The Koreans may have been defeated by the Japanese on land but, once the Japanese were established on the peninsula, the Korean navy, under the command of Admiral Yi Sun Sin, began to cut their lines of communications. Admiral Yi is a national hero to both halves of Korea, and there are pictures of him and models of his 'turtle-ships' in Seoul and P'yong-yang. This plate is based on a splendid painting in the Central Historical Museum in P'yong-yang, and an excellent model of the ship. *The Samurai – a Military History* by the present author contains a full account of the naval battles of the Korean War and a discussion of the tactics of the turtle boat which are illustrated here. A sulphurous smokescreen was emitted from the dragon's head in the bow and cannon lined its sides.

The Japanese warship looks very primitive by comparison. Kuroda Nagamasa stands bravely in the stern and is instantly recognisable by his buffalo-horn helmet. It is similar to that shown in Plate 14, and is illustrated in colour in *The Book of the Samurai* by the present author.

The Korean War

Nobunaga's motto had been *tenka fubu*, 'the realm covered in military glory'. To Hideyoshi this 'realm' extended far beyond the shores of Japan itself. His invasion of Korea, which had as its goal the eventual conquest of China, is a unique episode in samurai history. At no other time did the samurai attempt to conquer another country.

The first invasion sailed in 1592, and three columns under Konishi Yukinaga, a Christian *daimyo*, Kato Kiyomasa of the Nichiren Buddhist sect and Kuroda Nagamasa, marched up the Korean peninsula, carrying all before them. In almost every aspect of military behaviour the Japanese were superior. They were well supplied with firearms, had excellent field organisation, and the finest swords in the world. But the failure of the Korean army to stop them was not a failure shared by the Korean navy. Under the inspired command of Admiral Yi Sun Sin a fleet of heavily armed warships cut the Japanese lines of communication, and kept up relentless pressure on the supply of men and stores. Some of these ships, the famous 'turtle boats', were reinforced with iron plates. In time the pressure began to tell and, when China entered the war on the side of Korea, the Japanese became bogged down in a number of long sieges from which they had little hope of being relieved.

A second attempt was made in 1596, but this was brought to an end by Hideyoshi's death. The Korean War was therefore Hideyoshi's last campaign and ended a brilliant military career on a note of failure.

The *wakizashi*, the shorter of the pair of swords carried by samurai. This example, from a private collection, is of the Edo Period, and makes a *dai-sho* pair with the longer, but otherwise identical, *katana*.

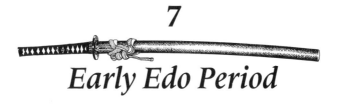

7

Early Edo Period

The last of the traditional pre-modern historical eras of Japan is known as the Edo, or Tokugawa Period, Edo from the city that grew from the town Ieyasu chose as his home, and Tokugawa from Ieyasu's surname, as his family supplied a long line of Shoguns who ruled Japan for two and a half centuries.

The Triumph of Tokugawa Ieyasu

'Nobunaga piled the rice, Hideyoshi kneaded the dough, while Tokugawa Ieyasu ate the cake,' says the old Japanese summary of the relative contribution to samurai history of the three unifiers. Hideyoshi in fact left a cake much nearer to completion when he died in 1598, but he died in the way that all dictators dread, leaving an infant son to inherit.

The political situation that was finally to be resolved at the Battle of Sekigahara in 1600 had an eerie echo of 1582, and Nobunaga's sudden

Corner tower and moat of the castle of Okazaki. Okazaki, on the Tokaido Road, was the birthplace of Tokugawa Ieyasu, and the chief town of Mikawa Province, home of the renowned 'Mikawa-bushi', of whom Ieyasu was their finest example.

Honda Heihachiro Tadakatsu, the companion of Tokugawa Ieyasu in all his battles, and a fine example of the spirit of the Mikawa-bushi. This statue of Tadakatsu wearing his famous stag's antler crest and huge wooden Buddhist rosary, stands in the grounds of Okazaki castle.

PLATE 26   *A Christian samurai, receives a blessing, ca 1596*

A Christian samurai, wearing a *namban-do*, an amalgam of European and Japanese armour, receives a blessing from a European priest before setting out for battle.

The enthusiasm for things European in the third quarter of the sixteenth century rarely extended beyond the acquisition of military equipment. This samurai has seen the quality of the stout European breastplate, and has had his armour-maker adapt it by drilling holes along its lower edge to take the suspensory cords for the skirt pieces, or *kusazuri*. He has also fitted a neckguard and 'browguard' to a morion-style helmet, which has been reversed for convenience in the operation.

The armour is based on several extant specimens in Japan of which the best known is the one preserved in the museum of the Toshogu Shrine at Nikko, which is supposed to have been worn by Tokugawa Ieyasu at the Battle of Sekigahara, and an almost identical suit in the Wakayama Toshogu Shrine. The priest is taken from one of the meticulously detailed figures of Europeans on the *'Namban Byobu'*, or 'Screen of the Southern Barbarians' in the museum at Kobe.

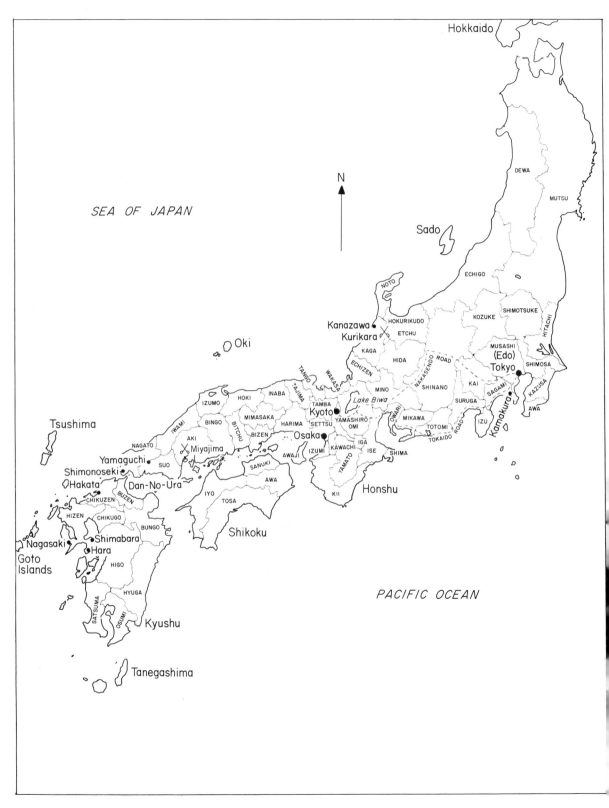

SEA OF JAPAN

N

Hokkaido

DEWA

MUTSU

Sado

ECHIGO

SHIMOTSUKE

KOZUKE

HITACHI

Kanazawa
Kurikara

HOKURIKUDO

ETCHU

KAGA

HIDA

NAKASENDO ROAD

SHINANO

MUSASHI
(Edo)
Tokyo

SHIMOSA

ECHIZEN

MINO

KAI

SAGAMI

KAZUSA

Kamakura

NOTO

TANGO

WAKASA

Lake Biwa

SURUGA

IZU

AWA

Oki

IZUMO

HOKI

INABA

TAJIMA

OWARI

MIKAWA

TOTOMI

TOKAIDO

ROAD

TAMBA

Kyoto

IWAMI

BINGO

MIMASAKA

HARIMA

SETTSU

YAMASHIRO
OMI

ISE

SHIMA

Tsushima

AKI

BITCHU

BIZEN

Osaka

IZUMI

KAWACHI

IGA

NAGATO

Miyajima

SANUKI

AWAJI

YAMATO

Yamaguchi

SUO

AWA

Honshu

Shimonoseki

Hakata

Dan-No-Ura

IYO

KII

CHIKUZEN

BUZEN

TOSA

Shikoku

HIZEN

CHIKUGO

BUNGO

Nagasaki

Shimabara
Hara

Goto
Islands

HIGO

PACIFIC OCEAN

HYUGA

SATSUMA

OSUMI

Kyushu

Tanegashima

death at the hands of a rival. Once again there was a power vacuum, and once again the strong rushed to fill it. It soon became obvious that the fight was to be largely between Eastern and Western Japan – East in the person of Tokugawa Ieyasu and West represented by Ishida Mitsunari, who was allied to a number of very powerful clans, including the Mori of the Inland Sea.

Ieyasu was 58 years old in 1600. He had lived a samurai life since childhood. As a young man he had been very nearly killed in battle by an arquebus ball fired by a warrior monk. He had felt the impact of the shot, but did not discover what a narrow escape he had had until later, when he stripped off his armour and a bullet fell out of his shirt. He had been one of Imagawa Yoshimoto's followers prior to the Battle of Okehazama, and joined Nobunaga after it. It was Ieyasu who had taken Nobunaga's frontier fortress of Marune, making good use of concentrated arquebus fire. Since then he had matured from a spear-swinging, fanatical samurai to a calm, self-possessed leader of men, a veteran of Mikata-ga-Hara, Nagashino, Nagakute and Odawara. The fiasco of the Korean War was the only major engagement of Hideyoshi's reign in which he did not serve. Once the great man was gone it was time for Ieyasu to seize power. Unlike either Nobunaga or Hideyoshi he had no obligation to rule merely as Regent. He was a Minamoto, the Shogun family, and everyone knew it.

Sekigahara was his Waterloo. By cleverly threatening Ishida's lines of communication to the East, Ieyasu drew him into a pitched battle on ground of his own choosing, at the most strategically placed crossroads in Japan. Sekigahara divides Japan in two. This little village nestling beneath Mount Ibuki, where streams poured down from the hillsides, was the setting for the mighty confrontation one October morning, when the fog

---

PLATE 27   *The Tokugawa army assaults Osaka castle in 1615*

Following the spurious peace treaty that ended temporarily the 'Winter Campaign' of Osaka castle, Tokugawa Ieyasu's army redoubled their efforts to destroy this mighty fortress in the *Osaka natsu no jin*, the Summer Campaign of Osaka, the last pitched battle between samurai armies. Here the Tokugawa troops go into action against one sector of Osaka's massive walls that survived even the blitz of 1945. Several of the clans allied to, or subservient to, the Tokugawa, are seen here. The *ashigaru* of the Ii family, ever-loyal supporters of the Tokugawa, are instantly recognisable by their red-lacquered armour. Two *ashigaru* of the Date family, wearing three little *sashimono* with one of Date Masamune's *mon* fire their arquebuses from behind the protection of a mobile shield. Its defence is a series of bundles of green bamboo, with gun slits cut through. They wear the now familiar *okegawa-do*.

The samurai dashing into the moat also wear the familiar battledress of *okegawa-do* and *zunari-kabuto*. Their *sashimono* have the *mon* of the Honda.

Also visible on the Tokugawa side are the troops of Uesugi Kagekatsu, whose submission to Tokugawa Ieyasu is now complete. They carry the red-rising-sun-on-blue flag that was the treasure of their house, under which marched the samurai of the great Uesugi Kenshin. Their *sashimono* have a design of lovebirds in bamboo.

Inside the walls we see the banners of Sanada Yukimura, identical to those of his grandfather shown in Plate 15. Yukimura was the great hero of Osaka, and is personally credited with wounding Tokugawa Ieyasu during the siege. The yellow banners with the Oda *mon* provide a strange link with the past. They indicate the presence in the castle of Oda Yuraku, brother of Nobunaga and a noted master of the arts of the tea ceremony. The other *nobori* banners belong to Goto Mototsugu of Kyushu.

Cannon were never fully developed by the samurai. These examples at Sekigahara, with the author standing next to them to indicate the size of the barrels, are actually made of wood and bound with thick ropes of twisted bamboo. Such examples must have been little more than fireworks. It was left to the bronze and iron specimens imported from Europe to blast the stone castles of the Momoyama Period.

made it dark as night. The battle was fought through mud and rain by the largest armies then assembled in a field battle. The Tokugawa faction were ultimately victorious and Sekigahara marked the beginning of an immense upheaval for everyone.

It did not, however, mark the end of Hideyoshi's line. Although Ieyasu was proclaimed Shogun, Hideyoshi's son was still alive and, in 1614, Hideyori, now grown to manhood, packed his late father's masterpiece of Osaka castle with sympathisers ranging from embittered Christians to dispossessed *daimyo*. The castle held out until the following summer and was only then taken by means of a trick whereby the defenders were made to agree to a reduction in size of the moats. Even then it did not fall until a huge pitched battle had been fought outside its walls. This battle, the Battle of Tenno-ji, became what Sekigahara is often thought to be – the last field battle between armies of samurai. Ieyasu, now an old man, took part in the actual fighting and is believed to have been wounded by a spear thrust near the kidneys. The Tokugawa triumph was no pushover.

The New Shogun

So a new era began. Another generation learnt to use the word Shogun, and old people reminded their grandchildren of what the title meant. For the samurai it was an unexpected revolution. Even before the last body was carted from the dark valley of Sekigahara, Ieyasu was planning his future, drawing on all the lessons he had seen and experienced over 50 years of samurai warfare. First, there had to be no rebellions by the lower classes, and Hideyoshi's Sword Hunt, by which he had disarmed all the non-samurai classes, had all but ensured that.

Secondly, there had to be no rebellions by samurai, and this was not to be left to chance. As a rule of thumb he divided the *daimyo* into those who had supported him at Sekigahara and those who had opposed him. The strongest among the latter were given fiefs at the ends of Japan, if not the

Details of horse equipment
As noted in the text, basic horse furniture changed appreciably little throughout samurai history, but this illustration shows a horse of the early Edo Period with full 'campaign equipment' of fodder bags, supplies for the rider and a holster for a matchlock pistol.

123

ends of the earth. The former found themselves suddenly quite wealthy, and living in strategic provinces close to the main lines of communication. The waverers found themselves comfortably off and in possession of their own heads, which was a decided improvement on Nobunaga's treatment of any who did not rush to embrace him.

The third Tokugawa Shogun, Iemitsu, extended Ieyasu's principle by requiring all the *daimyo* also to maintain a residence in Edo, and actually live there, next to the Shogun's palace, one year in two, with their wives and children staying in Edo permanently. The *daimyo* were astounded, for even Nobunaga's bold innovations had not stretched to taking hostages from every samurai family in Japan. Yet everyone complied, for such was the power of the new Shogunate.

Ieyasu's earlier reforms set in motion a furious spate of castle-building and moving house. One Japanese historian likened Ieyasu's *daimyo* to potted plants, that were uprooted and taken to flourish elsewhere. But there was a positive side to it. Ieyasu consciously strove to maintain and preserve the best features of *daimyo* rule as his system of local government, in the form of the *baku-han* system, whereby government was shared between the *bakufu* and the *daimyo* territories or *han*. Many of the *han* had been well administered, and it was a mark of Ieyasu's wise statesmanship that such a system could be allowed to continue.

In fact the control of the other *daimyo* by the Tokugawa family was so successful that it lasted for two and a half centuries, with little of the attendant rebellion that had plagued the Ashikaga or the Hojo *shikken*. One extraordinary feature of the Tokugawa *bakufu*'s relations with the *daimyo* is that never during the whole of the Edo Period were the *daimyo* subject to taxation by the central government. Instead the *bakufu* contrived

PLATE 28   *Tachibana Muneshige in camp, 1600*

Tachibana Muneshige (1567–1642) lived, and largely prospered, through some of the most tumultuous years of the Azuchi-Momoyama and Edo Periods. In 1587 he helped Hideyoshi in his defeat of the Shimazu clan of Kyushu and received a large grant of lands. He took part in the expedition to Korea and, together with Kobayakawa Takakage, gained a victory over a Chinese army. Later he was one of the *daimyo* who rescued Kato Kiyomasa from the siege of Uru-san. On his return to Japan his fortunes changed. He backed the wrong horse at Sekigahara and was dispossessed, but was restored to favour with the Tokugawa in 1611 and took part in the suppression of the Shimabara revolt at the ripe old age of 71.

He is seen here peering over the top the *maku*, the curtains that customarily surrounded a general's field headquarters, which bear his ornate *mon*. A retainer holds the even more ornate banner of Tachibana Muneshige, which bears the discs of the sun and the moon on either side of a *bonji*, a Sanskrit character. The inscription reads 'Tenshoko Daijin', i.e. the Goddess of the Sun, Amateratsu Omikami, divine ancestress of the Emperors of Japan.

His helmet is a simple *zunari-kabuto* with a *shikoro* laced in blue *sugake-odoshi*. Once again, this simple design has been given some ornamentation, in his case in the form of a 'halo', and a plume of cock's feathers.

Next to him stands a young page. The boy has not yet performed his *gembuku*, or 'manhood ceremony', which would be accompanied by the shaving of the long forelock of hair which he has fastened back with his pigtail. The unshaven forelock was regarded as being very attractive on a youth. Nevertheless the boy is in full armour, and is prepared to play his part on the field of battle.

All the details are based on actual specimens, and the Tachibana family records.

to keep the *daimyo* in a constant state of genteel poverty. They were obliged to make generous donations towards the building and upkeep of the Shogun's fortresses of Edo, Osaka, Nagoya and Nijo (in Kyoto), which included the supplying and transportation of men and materials. Much of these materials consisted of huge blocks of stone, so castle-building became a constant drain on finance and manpower.

Communication in Edo Japan

It is also not generally realised just how difficult transport was in Japan until comparatively modern times, a factor that has considerable bearing on samurai history. Accounts of journeys made during the Edo Period make the 'horror stories' of stagecoach driving in eighteenth-century England, with its muddy, potholed roads and lurking highwaymen, seem positively luxurious. Transport along the Shogun's highways followed routes determined almost totally by accidents of geography. Such roads that existed were far from continuous, being cut many times along their length by rivers, of which few were bridged. In fact during the Edo Period the number of bridges across Japanese rivers actually decreased as difficulty in communication was seen as a hindrance to potential rebellion.

Examples of the simple wheeled carts used for transportation purposes in the towns and in the countryside. The example on the right is laden with bales made of rice-straw. (Toei-Uzumasa Film Studios, Kyoto)

126

So, once peace was established by Ieyasu, bridges were allowed to fall into disrepair and the accepted means of crossing a swollen river was to be carried on the shoulders of the burly tattooed porters, whose livelihood was this unusual form of ferry service. When on the roads, personal transport was either a horse, a *kago*, or palanquin, ranging from a simple litter to an elaborately shuttered, lacquered version, or one's own two feet. Wheeled traffic was completely banned from the Tokaido, the Great East Sea Road that linked Kyoto and Edo, because of the damage it would do to the surface. In fact the only wheeled vehicles to be seen anywhere were the traditional ox-carriages used by the Imperial Court for their short journeys in Kyoto, various farm carts and the decorated wagons for shrine festivals.

Such considerations give one a greater respect for the achievements of men like Hideyoshi in actually moving their colossal armies from place to place. We must remember, however, that the decline in transportation systems only set in once wars had ceased. In Hideyoshi's call-to-arms, addressed to Tokugawa Ieyasu prior to the siege of Odawara, he commands his ally to repair all bridges along the Tokaido and build new ones.

With such apparent difficulties it is astonishing to learn that the major highways of Japan were always teeming with people moving from place to place. The major reason for this was the Shogun Tokugawa Iemitsu's

The most welcome sight for a samurai travelling along one of the main highways of Japan on a *daimyo*'s procession to or from the Shogun's capital at Edo was a post-station, where lodgings could be obtained for the night. This is the Magome Honjin, the official post-station in the village of Magome, an important stop on the old road through the central mountains that linked Kyoto and Edo.

The Taiko-mon, or Drum Gate, of Hikone Castle
Hikone is a good example of the castles that were built during the Early Edo Period. This old photograph shows the *Taiko-mon*, with its guard house built over the stout wooden doors.

sankin-kotai, or Alternate Attendance System. Reference has been made above to the dual residence requirement forced upon the *daimyo*. The other feature of the *sankin-kotai* was that, when the *daimyo* changed their residence from Edo to provincial capital or back again, they did so accompanied by a splendid retinue of samurai, gorgeously dressed and fully equipped for the Shogun's service. As most of the *daimyo* had to do this trip in one direction or another every single year it ensured a continual financial commitment, an infallible hostage system, and an opportunity for the Shogun's staff to keep themselves fully informed on any gossip from the provinces.

An alternative to road transport were journeys by river or sea, a need which grew with the expanding economy of the Edo Period. A pack horse could only carry two bales of rice and, as the years went by, *daimyo* had an

PLATE 29   *Hosokawa Tadaoki (1564–1645) has his sword tested during a lull in the fighting in the siege of Osaka*

Tadaoki was the grandson of a certain Mibuchi Harusada, whose surname he used until the time of Sekigahara. Mibuchi Harusada had been adopted into the Hosokawa family, whose earlier illustrious members are illustrated in Plate 13. Tadaoki served under the three unifiers of Japan. Nobunaga gave him Tango Province in 1580, and he remained loyal to Nobunaga in spite of being married to Akechi Mitsuhide's daughter. In 1590 he took part in the Odawara campaign and besieged Nirayama castle on

Hideyoshi's behalf. At the time of Sekigahara Ishida Mitsunari took many daimyo's families as hostages in Osaka castle, hoping thereby to force them to support him against Ieyasu. Among them was Tadaoki's Christian wife, Gracia, who had been baptised in 1587. Tadaoki stood firm against Ishida's threats, but it cost his wife her life. He took part in the Battle of Sekigahara and the siege of Osaka castle.

Tadaoki had a fondness for ornamenting his helmets with feathers. He is described as having a

pheasant's tail in his helmet at Sekigahara. Here he sports peacock's plumes out of a straightforward *zunari-kabuto*. The armour, and the swords, are modelled on the actual specimens.

The testing of his sword on the corpse of an executed criminal has been done by a *hinin*, a person of outcast status, forced to work in the execution grounds. Around him are the remains of those defeated by the Tokugawa armies. The *nobori* banner bears the *mon* of the Hosokawa.

increasing need to ship vast quantities of their crop to the cities of Edo and Osaka to convert it into cash. River transport had been used for centuries, but few river journeys could be accomplished without considerable stretches overland. For example, in 1638 an experiment was undertaken whereby rice from Kaga Province was taken by land to the Northern shore of Lake Biwa. It was then ferried by boat to Otsu and on down the Yodo River to Osaka. By the end of the seventeenth century a 'shuttle service' of rice-ships had been established between the rice-growing areas of Northern Japan and the cities of Edo and Osaka. One voyage sailed along the Pacific Coast to Edo. The other went South-West through the Sea of Japan, passed through the Straits of Shimonoseki, and sailed up the Inland Sea to Osaka.

A youth of the samurai class
This actor from the Toei-Uzumasa studios in Kyoto is dressed in typical fashion for the period. He wears *hakama*, and has a short *haori* over his *kimono*. He carries a bamboo and paper umbrella.

The Shimabara Rebellion

Reference was made in the previous chapter to the virtual suppression of Christianity under the Tokugawa *bakufu*. The expulsion of Christian samurai such as Takayama Ukon was merely one stage in the process. The final hardening of the Tokugawa attitude came after an insurrection in 1638 known as the Shimabara Rebellion, a rising small in itself, but one that produced repercussions at a national and international level.

130

Tokugawa Ieyasu
First of the Tokugawa Shoguns and the victor of Sekigahara, Tokugawa Teyasu is a vital figure in Japanese history. This fine statue of him is in the grounds of Okazaki Castle, where Ieyasu was born in 1542. His suit of armour is very similar to the one he is.supposed to have worn at Nagakute.

A samurai wearing a haori
An actor from the Toei-Uzumasa film studios wearing a very unpretensious *haori*.

131

The *daimyo* of the Shimabara peninsula was Matsukura Shigeharu, whose methods of dealing with people who were suspected of being Christians were among the cruellest in the savage history of the persecutions. A favourite torture of his was to lower his prisoners into the boiling, sulphurous hot springs of Unzen until they were scalded to death. The revolt against him broke out in Shimabara on 17 December 1637 and was led by a group of *shoya,* village headmen, who had formerly served under Christian *daimyo* such as Konishi Yukinaga. One outstanding feature of the rebellion is that, from very early on, it became a decidedly Christian affair, even though the motives may have been as much economic as religious. The nominal commander was a youth called Amakusa Shiro, who comes over as something of a 'Joan of Arc' character, acting as an inspiration for the cause and playing the part of a figurehead for the army.

What is more surprising is the sluggishness of the *bakufu's* response. Part was due no doubt to the communication difficulties discussed above, which were particularly severe in the case of journeys to Kyushu. The trip from Edo took 6 days overland to Osaka followed by 10 days on board ship, so a rapid response from Edo was physically impossible. Local help was ruled out because of the Tokugawa regulations forbidding intercourse between neighbouring *han,* even to the extent of preventing them from assisting one another in this sort of circumstance. So two neighbouring armies sat idly by as the revolt spread around the peninsula while the regulatory mechanisms which the *bakufu* had proudly set up to contain such rebellions prevented any action from being taken.

The rebels thus began well and took everything in their stride. Soon they controlled half the Shimabara peninsula, but their attempt to take the mighty Shimabara castle failed, and, faced with the approach of a *bakufu* army, their leadership decided to fortify the abandoned castle of Hara at the Southern end of the peninsula. Here they withstood a long siege against a veteran warrior called Itakura Shigemasa, who had been generously rewarded for his actions during the great siege of Osaka in 1615. His conduct of this siege was, however, so inept that the *bakufu* were forced to send considerable reinforcements, which mortified him. Itakura then launched an ill-prepared attack designed to capture Hara castle before the

PLATE 30   *A townsman defeats a samurai in unarmed combat, ca 1630*

A townsman uses unarmed combat techniques to defeat an armed samurai. Although the wearing of the two swords was restricted to the samurai class these swaggering warriors did not always have it their own way. Many stories tell of bands of *chonin* (townspeople) in cities such as Edo or Osaka who joined together in gangs to defeat unscrupulous samurai.

Both parties in this tussle are wearing *kimono,* a long garment like a dressing gown, underneath a pair of wide *hakama* (trousers). *Hakama* fastened first with a pair of straps from front to back, which were concealed by the stiffened flap at the back, and a pair of tying cords secured neatly at the front. The swords were thrust into these belts.

others arrived, but it was beaten off to the jeers of the defenders.

On Lunar New Year's Day 1638, Itakura tried again, and led the first charge himself until he was killed by an arrow. The loss of the commander shocked the *bakufu*. If a band of peasants and Christians could do this to the mighty Tokugawa war machine, what might an experienced *daimyo*, with a samurai army, hope to achieve? So far the siege was acting just like Kusunoki Masashige's famous defence of Chihaya. It showed their weakness, and invited imitation.

The Tokugawa troops were in an embarrassing state, and at one stage got so desperate that they asked a Dutch ship to bombard the castle for them, but the moral disgrace of having to depend upon foreigners negated any military advantage. All the besiegers could hope for was to starve the defenders out before any one else joined their rebellion, or any similar actions started elsewhere in Japan. Such a siege required patience, but as the weeks went by the strategy began to pay off. The capture of some rebels out on a sortie confirmed that food supplies were running very low. Soon came the final assault. It was carefully planned, but began prematurely when a signal fire was lit by mistake. Soon thousands of samurai poured into the attack in a disorganised charge, each trying to gain as much personal glory as possible by being the first into the attack. The castle fell, but not without considerable loss to the attackers.

Shimabara was a portent of the samurai decline. The all-conquering Tokugawa army had been shown to be susceptible to rebellion. Ieyasu thought he had controlled the *daimyo*, but the biggest challenge to his successors had come from a different direction. Shimabara also hastened the end of Christianity in Japan, and was followed within a few years by the closing of Japan to the outside world, which was to have such an effect on the country's later history. No foreign ship was allowed to land, except for a few Dutch who were confined to the island of Deshima in Nagasaki. No Japanese were allowed to leave, and any who did, and were foolish enough to return, were executed. From being an outgoing, adventurous nation whose samurai had visited and traded with the Philippines and Siam, Japan became deliberately isolated and turned its back on the world.

8

Later Edo Period

The Shimabara Rebellion marked the last serious attempt to defy the *bakufu* by force, and is an appropriate incident from which to continue our discussion of the role of the samurai in Tokugawa society during the period of seclusion.

The Urban Samurai

The need, discussed above, for supplying cities with rice arose out of the fact that the samurai of the Edo Period was essentially an urban creature. Nobunaga had begun the trend of separating the samurai from the soil when he disciplined his *ashigaru* and treated them as regular soldiers with smart uniforms and the opportunity for promotion. Hideyoshi, who had begun his glorious career as a humble *ashigaru*, accelerated the trend by encouraging the growth of castle towns and disarming the peasantry by his Sword Hunt, until in the Edo Period there was a very clear distinction between samurai and farmer. The samurai class, of whom the *ashigaru* were now the lowest ranks, lived in the castle towns alongside the merchants and craftsmen, and fought for their *daimyo* on the Shogun's behalf, when there was anything to fight about.

PLATE 31   *A samurai leads his contingent to serve the Shogun, ca 1650*

Throughout the period under discussion the wealth of a samurai, assessed in *koku*, (one *koku* was about 180 litres) provided the basis whereby the feudal service he was required to provide to his overlord might be assessed. The most important set of such regulations were set out by the Tokugawa Shogun in 1629 and remained in force, with little modification, until the end of the Tokugawa Period. Using the requirements for a samurai whose wealth was valued at 200 *koku* (theoretically enough rice to feed 200 men for 1 year), we have therefore invented this imaginary samurai, who is making his unhurried way along the Tokaido Road to serve the Shogun. Besides his personal service, mounted, he supplies for the Shogun's use one samurai on foot, who has just returned from a successful foraging expedition, one armour-bearer (who carries a large lacquered box on his back, containing the lord's helmet, and perhaps a spare suit of armour), one spearman, one groom and one baggage-carrier.

In the space of a very few years, such processions across Japan were to lose all martial connotations and become the biennial journey to pay respects to the Shogun, under Tokugawa Iemitsu's *sankin-kotai*, or 'Alternate Attendance System'.

Note the *hachimaki*, or headbands worn by the two samurai, augmented with a portion of chain mail. The armour is *okegawa-do*.

Within these towns and cities the samurai class constituted the majority of the population. In Sendai, the castle town of the *daimyo* Date Masamune, samurai formed 70 per cent of the inhabitants, while in Kagoshima the proportion was the largest – about 80 per cent. By contrast, in the country as a whole, the samurai were always the minority, probably no more than 7 per cent of the population, but a minority that wielded enormous power.

While the samurai lived in towns the farmers lived in the countryside and grew the food. That at any rate was the theory, though there was a 'grey area' between the two classes, where one finds the *shoya*, the village headmen, who could possess enormous local power, and various 'country samurai'. There were also the notorious *ronin*. A *ronin* (the name means 'man of the waves') was a samurai who had become dispossessed owing to the death or disgrace of his master. Some *ronin* could find employment with other *daimyo*, but as their trade was warfare such opportunities decreased with the establishment of the Tokugawa Shogunate, apart from their roles as 'hired swords' so beloved of the Japanese movie industry. But the poverty which the *ronin* experienced was to some extent shared by all low-ranking samurai. They were paid a fixed stipend in a world of rising prices, but were required to maintain themselves and their followers in true samurai style, fully equipped and armed, and always ready for battle muster. Detailed regulations existed which laid down the number of men and their equipment which samurai of a certain rank would be required to supply in times of war. Promotion was limited once battles had ceased, so many samurai turned to trade and handicrafts to make ends meet. Farming

A swordsman
This illustration by the artist Hokusai depicts a samurai drawing his sword, perhaps to take part in a street brawl. He may well be a *ronin*, a samurai without a master to serve.

A cart laden with rice bales
A photo from the Toei-Uzumasa film studios depicting one variety of cart used during the Edo Period.

138

and umbrella-making are among the occupations of the 'black economy' listed for samurai.

At the same time the world of the castle town was one that put endless temptations in their way, all of which cost money. The growing wealth of the merchant classes encouraged various forms of entertainment to flourish, including the *kabuki* theatre, which was officially banned to the samurai class, but much patronised by them. *Kabuki* was to the vulgar townsmen what the stately *noh* plays were to the noble samurai: a form of theatrical art that mirrored the lives they led. While the sons of *daimyo* sat motionless through the stylised re-telling of the deeds of their tragic and honourable ancestors, the citizens screamed, shouted and rolled in the

A prominent sight in any town in the Edo Period was the watchtower, from which fires could be readily spotted and attended to. This reconstruction is part of the Toei-Uzumasa Film Studios in Kyoto.

aisles as a *kabuki* troup re-enacted a fight between townsmen and samurai, a love-suicide of a merchant's daughter, or a farmer outwitting his superior. It was brash, gaudy, emotionally unrestrained, and blatantly counter to the moral standards of the Shogun, all of which attracted the samurai in droves. *Kabuki* was banned several times, but all attempts at curtailing it proved ineffective.

The gradual neglect of the martial arts in favour of office work, the need for supplementary trades, and the lure of townsmen's pleasures produced an economic effect far beyond the official boundaries of the samurai class. If the suppliers of credit, prostitutes and theatres were the new profiteers, the older craftsmen, such as swordsmiths, suffered with their former patrons. A poignant example is recorded for the swordsmiths of Kanazawa. At the time of the foundation of the Kaga *han* there had been a great demand for their skills. Maeda Toshitsune (1593–1658) once placed an order for five *katana* and 650 *yari* (spears), the order being fulfilled by seven swordsmiths. One good sword by the leading Kaga swordsmith, Kiyomitsu Shichiemon, could cost the equivalent of one *koku* in wages, plus materials (The *koku* was the amount of rice considered necessary to feed one man for 1 year) and Kiyomitsu was used to receiving orders for up to twenty *katana* at any one time. Yet, within two generations, his grandson Chobei was forced by poverty to the poorhouse, where he continued to make one or two swords.

An actor at the Toei-Uzumasa Film Studios in Kyoto showing the typical samurai hairstyle, whereby the front half of the head was shaved bare and the rest of the hair was gathered into a pigtail which was oiled and tied up.

In 1720 the *daimyo* of Kanazawa placed an order for swords, but the swordsmith chosen had to look up old records to find out what price to ask. Many of the swordsmiths by then made more money from making pots and pans, and petitioned the City Magistrates to allow them to gather firewood. 'There have been no orders for swords from the *han* or from the samurai...', they wrote. 'We are starving and our business prospects are poor.'

Swordsmiths were only one of the many tradesmen who came under the heading of *chonin*, or townspeople, whose lives were regulated by the samurai. There were rules for practically everything and some of the following, a selection from regulations published in Kanazawa in 1642, show an admirable, if somewhat paternalistic concern for public health and safety:

PLATE 32   *A ninja prepares to kill a victim, ca 1640*

A *ninja* assassin, dressed in black, prepares to leap down through the gap he has made in the ceiling onto his terrified victim. *Ninja* dressed almost all in black for night work and in a khaki-brown garment during daylight hours. The costume is based on exhibits in the Ninja Museum at Iga-Ueno. As the art of the assassin was one of secrecy it is questionable how much of 'ninja-lore' is authentic, but no book on samurai would be complete without them!

Chonin, regardless of who they are, will be held responsible if they are slovenly or commit improprieties towards samurai.

It is forbidden to keep dogs as pets or to walk along the street next to samurai

Chonin are not to gather in shops and gossip loudly about others, nor are chonin in shops to sit around in rude positions.

Persons who urinate from the second floor of houses in the city, regardless of whether it is night or day, shall certainly be punished. If a traveller at an inn commits such an act the innkeeper shall be held responsible. This is to be explained to all children, travellers, and persons of low status. Spitting from the second floor, throwing waste water from the second floor, and opening the second floor windows and staring at passers-by or calling out rude comments to them are also prohibited....

This was the Tokugawa Peace, a world based on the Confucian ideals of order and benevolent authority, where everyone knew his place and was in his place.

An actor at the Toei-Uzumasa Studios in the role of a samurai. He is wearing an ornate long-sleeved *haori*.

The Loyal Retainers

'Great Peace Throughout the Realm' was the aim and motto of the Tokugawa and, by and large, that peace was maintained for 250 years. In 1702 there occurred an incident which, in its own way, shocked the *bakufu* as much by its evidence of the continued existence of samurai values as the Shimabara Rebellion had shocked it by their apparent absence. The story is a classic of revenge and spawned hundreds of plays, prints and, more recently, films depicting the tale of the Forty-Seven Ronin.

Secret signs of the ninja
This wax dummy in the Ninja Museum in Iga-Ueno shows a samurai making the secret signs associated with the "invisible men", the famous *ninja*, that were supposed to confer great powers.

A daimyo's procession
This illustration depicts a daimyo's procession from the mid-nineteenth century, as may be inferred from the fixed bayonets carried by the samurai. Note the townsmen with their heads pressed tightly to the ground.

142

The *daimyo* whose death made his retainers into *ronin* was Asano Naganori (1667–1701), who owned a *han* worth 50,000 *koku* in Harima Province. He was one of two *daimyo*, then on their periodic visit to Edo, who had been selected to entertain representatives of the Emperor at the Shogun's Court – a very great honour. The other *daimyo*, Kira Yoshinaka, was charged with instructing Asano in the correct behaviour, but when his pupil failed to present him with the customary gifts he became abusive and scornful. On one occasion he criticised Asano in public, causing the other to lose his temper, and wounded Kira on the forehead with his *wakizashi*. Even to draw a weapon in the Shogun's presence was a serious offence, and Asano was made to commit *hara-kiri*. His forty-seven samurai, who had now been made *ronin*, plotted Kira's death as revenge. What is extraordinary about the story is the fantastic lengths to which they went in order to make Kira think that they had all split up, had no communication with each other, and had all abandoned the profession of samurai. Their leader, Oishi Yoshio, even divorced his wife, and kept up a facade of drunken, dissolute pleasure-seeking. One snowy night in December 1702 the *ronin*, dressed in home-made armour, struck at Kira's mansion in Edo.

The attack was a masterpiece of military organisation which would have done credit to a modern-day SAS. operation. Twenty-three attacked from the rear, while the rest approached from the front. A small group climbed the wall with rope ladders, but being unable to obtain any keys from the terrified guards they smashed the gate down with a mallet. While some of the *ronin* stationed themselves outside with bows, to cut down anyone fleeing, the others broke into the house itself and started searching for Kira. He and his followers are often depicted as craven cowards to contrast them with the gallant *ronin*, but in fact he was well defended by samurai as loyal as the forty-seven. Three of his samurai held the *ronin* off from Kira's quarters for some considerable time.

Kira Yoshinaka was eventually found hiding in an outhouse. He was first invited to commit *hara-kiri*, but as there was a danger of a counter-attack

PLATE 33   *The Shogun Tokugawa Yoshimune leads manoeuvres in 1720*

The energetic Shogun Tokugawa Yoshimune (reigned from 1716 to 1745) produced many reforms in the Shogunate, and made a valiant attempt to revive the martial accomplishments of his ancestors. Mock battles and manoeuvres were conducted on the plains below Mount Fuji, and in this picture we see the Shogun himself, wearing the elaborate armour that is preserved in the Kunozan Toshogu Shrine Museum in Shizuoka.

The armour is a classic of its kind. It is basically a revival *yoroi* – but what a revival! No expense has been spared in ornamenting it to a standard even more exquisite than the old *yoroi* shown in Plates 1 to 8, with which it is instructive to compare this specimen. It has a sixteenth-century *mempo*, with a handlebar moustache, and an enormous *yodarekake*. The helmet is a graceful *sujibachi*. The *haidate* are of a later model, but the *suneate* are big and heavy. His *tachi* sword is bejewelled and very ornate. The samurai behind him wear the style of *jingasa* helmets with steeper conical bowls than those that are found in earlier times. Their 'battledress' stands in marked contrast to their leader, whose armour was not made for real fighting.

Front, side and rear views of the formal samurai dress known as the *kami-shimo* ('upper and lower'), which consisted of the more usual *kimono* and *hakama* (wide trousers), but instead of the *haori*, as shown on page 142, a jacket called the *kataginu* was worn. The *kataginu* had stiffened shoulders, giving the costume its characteristic appearance, and would normally be of the same material as the *hakama*, as in the case of the dress of this actor at the Toei-Uzumasa Film Studios in Kyoto.

by Kira's supporters, Oishi cut off his head with the very dagger with which Asano had committed suicide and the raiders departed. By now all Edo was awake and the people crowded the streets to see the bizarre procession go by: forty-six bloodstained men (one had died during the raid) carrying a wooden bucket in which was Kira's head, making for the Sengaku-ji where Asano was buried, there to place the head on their master's tomb.

Their action placed the *bakufu* in a nice dilemma. Should they condemn the *ronin* for murder, and punish them, or reward them for their fidelity to the ideals of the samurai life? In the end the laws of the land had to take precedence and the remaining *ronin* committed suicide at Sengaku-ji, where they are buried, leaving behind them a noble legacy of samurai virtue that was never to be equalled.

The Fall of the Tokugawa

The forces that eventually overthrew the Tokugawa *bakufu* and laid the foundations of modern Japan did so in the name of an institution that was far older than that of the Shogun, and with a potential far greater for inspiring loyalty and nationalist feelings. The opposition to the Tokugawa came from men who rediscovered the magic in the name of the Emperor.

The impetus for their actions came from a very different direction than the simple loyalty that had inspired Kusunoki Masashige to die for the Emperor, or the promise of personal gain that had motivated some of his contemporaries. From the beginning of the nineteenth century there were frequent incursions into Japanese waters by foreign vessels and, when Commodore Perry's black ships sailed majestically into Tokyo Bay in 1854, it was seen that the power of the Western World was not something that could be ignored. The foreigners had either to be accepted or defied. The factor in this political turmoil that is so fascinating is that the Shogunate was overthrown by men who opposed opening up Japan to Western nations and saw the Shogun as a traitor in that he was signing treaties and entertaining embassies. At the same time, however, these men also saw, more clearly than the Shogun, that unless they absorbed the military

PLATE 34   *A Samurai guard kills an intruder in 1750*

In this plate a samurai uses his *wakizashi*, the shorter of the pair of swords normally carried, to kill a *ronin* (literally 'a man of the waves' – a samurai who has no master, and no income).

The samurai is wearing the *kami-*shimo, the formal attire of a *daimyo's* retainers. On top of the *kimono* shown in Plate 30 he wears a winged jacket with stiffened shoulders. He has probably left the longer of his swords in a sword rack, but sees the danger, and acts.

The *ronin* is a scruffy character, with untidy hair and rough-and-ready clothes. He too, has only a *wakizashi*, probably owing to poverty. His trousers are *ko-bakama*, the shorter form of *hakama*, tucked into gaiters.

lessons of the Western nations they could never hope to defeat them. Thus began a period of time which appears to a cursory glance to be an unbridled enthusiasm for anything Western. In fact a careful examination reveals that it was nothing of the sort. All the new materials, techniques and methods that the Japanese adopted had sound utilitarian considerations behind them, the most important of which was a desire eventually to use them against their providers. Thus the Japanese noted the use of military music on board ship following the British bombardment of Kagoshima in 1863. It was seen to be useful for morale – it would be useful for them.

But a feudal institution like the Shogunate was no longer appropriate. It had to be removed, and the name of the Emperor provided the focus around which such opposition could be organised, by appealing to something that was even more 'Japanese' than the Shogunate. The two most powerful *daimyo* at the time not related to the Tokugawa were those whose territories comprised Satsuma, at the Southern tip of Kyushu, and Choshu, at the Western end of Honshu. Both were *tozama*, the 'Outer Lords' of Ieyasu's reckoning, who had been placed under the watchful eye of pro-Tokugawa men. Both were equally opposed to foreign intercourse, and both were equally against the continuation of the Shogunate. Various outrages against foreigners by these *daimyo* complicated the Shogun's relations with foreigners in the capital and gave rise to claims for reparation which the Shogun could not refuse, but which lowered his prestige with his fellow countrymen. In 1863 Satsuma and Choshu prevailed upon the Emperor officially to expel the foreigners and forbid Japan's ports to them, a decree which both clans rushed to obey. We have noted one result of this action above – the bombardment of Kagoshima by British ships. A year later a combined fleet forced the Straits of Shimonoseki, between Kyushu and Choshu, and bombarded the Japanese forts. It was a harsh lesson for Satsuma and Choshu.

In 1866 the incumbent Shogun died, and was followed within a few months by the Emperor Komei. Their successors, Tokugawa Keiki and Emperor Mutsuhito (soon to be known as Meiji) were now new men at the helm, who realised that a nation divided against itself could not stand. The

---

PLATE 35   *The murder of Ii Naosuke by Imperial loyalists in 1860*

'Sonno-joi!' – 'Honour the Emperor and expel the barbarians!' – was the rallying cry of the factions opposed to the increased intercourse with Western nations that led to the opening of Japan to the world in the 1850s and 1860s. Ii Naosuke (1815–1860) the Shogun's chief minister, was the noblest victim to die at the hands of those who wished to resist the Western alliances by force.

He was murdered early one morning in March 1860. He had been travelling in a shuttered palanquin and was stopped by *ronin* from the Mito *daimyo*.

This plate is based on numerous contemporary illustrations of the shocking deed. The bearers have been depicted with the traditional tattoos sported by such men. The assassins run off in triumph with Naosuke's severed head, leaving his headless corpse behind. The guards wear the Ii *mon* on their *haori* jackets.

movement for the restoration of the ancient system of government by the Emperor grew in force until it was literally irresistible. In November 1867 the Shogun formally handed over to the Emperor the commission of Shogun which Minamoto Yoritomo had first received in 1192. For a while it seemed that the final step in the great revolution would be accomplished peacefully and that, once the Shogun had yielded, his followers would loyally copy his example. But it was not to be. Kyoto at the time was guarded by samurai from Aizu, in the North of Japan, tough, fanatical samurai whose fidelity to the Tokugawa Shoguns was legendary. They were ordered to surrender by the allied clans of Satsuma and Choshu, but refused to give in, and withdrew with the Shogun to Osaka. There the remaining adherents of the Tokugawa gathered, all bitter at the downfall of the Shogun and all determined not to give up without a final struggle. Their immediate anger turned against the Satsuma headquarters in Osaka, which consisted of a palace for the *daimyo* and barracks for the samurai. This was taken and burned, and then the whole Tokugawa force turned towards the capital. They were met by the Imperial forces near Fushimi, 7 miles to the South of Kyoto.

The Battle of Fushimi which ensued is often treated as a footnote in Japanese history, a minor inconvenience. In fact it was one of the most decisive battles in Japanese history and lasted longer than many of the great encounters of the Momoyama Period. It actually lasted for 3 days, from the 28 to the 30 of January 1868, and the Tokugawa troops were only

The Battle of Ueno on 4 July 1868 was the last encounter between the Imperial Troops and the last remnants of the Shogun's army. This contemporary print is preserved in the Memorial Shrine at Ueno.

The statue in Ueno Park of Saigo Takamori, whose doomed Satsuma Rebellion of 1877 made him the last of the samurai warriors.

154

defeated when one of their number, stationed on the left flank, deserted them for the Emperor. As they fled before the victors, the Shogun took a ship from Osaka to Edo, and his erstwhile supporters, as a last gesture of defiance, set fire to the palace built by Hideyoshi, the man whose family the Tokugawa had supplanted, within the walls of Osaka castle. Perhaps they had originally wished to suffer the fate of Hideyoshi's son and conduct a siege from Osaka itself? But they were broken. The Shogun, as we noted above, had been taken to Edo, where he formally surrendered the Eastern capital to the Emperor. Some stubborn Tokugawa loyalists retired to the North, where they held out for another 6 months. One small band made a last stand at Ueno, which is now part of Tokyo, and on 4 July 1868 were attacked by an overwhelming force of Imperial troops. The stubborn Tokugawa samurai fought to the last man.

With their collapse the Tokugawa resistance faded and the history of the samurai moved swiftly towards its close. One by one the edicts came. In 1871 the wearing of swords was made optional, and in 1876 it was banned altogether to everyone except members of the armed forces. One Satsuma samurai, Saigo Takamori, found it too much to stand and, in his native province, raised a rebellion against the new order. He was faced with, and destroyed by, the conscript army of the new Japan, whose modern rifles cut down Saigo's swordsmen. His inevitable defeat, and his heroic last stand which ended with his suicide, were no more than fitting for that final flowering of the spirit of the samurai which Saigo Takamori represents. With his death the samurai of real life passed away, to be replaced by the samurai warriors of myth and story, who have grown in stature as the years have gone by, always the heroes, ever noble and ever brave.

PLATE 36   *A komuso uses his flute against an assassin, ca 1790*

Amongst the strangest sights on the streets of Japan in the Edo Period were the wandering, flute-playing monks called *komuso*, a word that literally means 'monks of emptiness'. Their origin is something of a mystery, though members of the sect itself, the Fuke-shu, which is a branch of Zen, invented several spurious claims to ancestry, including descent from the Kusunoki clan. Their traditional wear consisted of a dark blue or black *kimono*, and a special sort of *kesa* worn over the left shoulder, but the most noticeable feature of dress is the remarkable *tengai*, the basket hat that entirely covered the head. The reeds were woven tightly everywhere except in front of the eyes, so that the wearer could not be identified, yet could view the world outside. A short sword was carried in a cloth bag tied with two cords that represented the principles of *yin* and *yang*. There were certain rituals about drawing the sword, and how combat should be conducted, though our example in this plate (as in so many Japanese movies) has not waited to draw his sword but has used his *shakuhachi* as a club. One recent commentator on the *komuso* noted that such practice 'would have led to a slight mistuning'!

The anonymity afforded by *komuso* garb led many *ronin* to adopt the *komuso* life unofficially, which probably gained the sect a bad name on several occasions.

The assailant in this picture has prepared for action. He has pulled up the skirts of his *hakama* and tucked them under his belt. His flowing sleeves have been tied back with the *tasuki* sash.

The traditions of the Fukeshu have been revived in the last century at the Myoan-ji in Kyoto, a sub-temple of the Tofuku-ji. The author visited the Myoan-ji in 1986, and it is on materials kindly supplied by the monks that this picture is based. The author also had the unusual privilege of meeting a present-day *komuso*, in full traditional costume, on a bus in Hiroshima.

Readers who are interested in learning more about the Fukeshu are referred to the excellent article by James H. Sanford in *Monumenta Nipponica*, volume 32, pp. 411–440.

Bibliography

References cited in the text and other recommended works:

Birt, M.P. *Warring States: A Study of the Go-Hojo Daimyo and Domain* Ph.D. Thesis, Princeton University 1983

Birt, M.P. 'Samurai in passage: the transformation of the sixteenth century Kanto' *Journal of Japanese Studies* 1985 **11:** 369–399

Brownlee, J.S. 'The Shokyu War and the political rise of the warriors' *Monumenta Nipponica* —— **24:** 59–77

Elison, G. & Smith, B.L. *Warlords, Artists and Commoners* University of Hawaii Press 1981

Hall, J.W. (ed.) *Japan Before Tokugawa* Princeton University Press 1981

Sanford, J.H. 'Shakuhachi zen' *Monumenta Nipponica* —— **32:** 411–440

Sasama, Y. *Zukai Nihon Katchu Jiten* Tokyo 1973

Sasama, Y. *Zuroko Nihon no Katchu Bugu Jiten* Tokyo 1978

Sugiyama, H. 'Sengoku daimyo' *Nihon no Rekishi* Vol. II Tokyo 1971

Turnbull, S.R. *The Samurai – A Military History* Osprey 1977

Turnbull, S.R. *Samurai Armies 1550–1615* Osprey 1979

Turnbull, S.R. *Warlords of Japan* Sampson Low 1979

Turnbull, S.R. *The Mongols* Osprey 1980

Turnbull, S.R. *The Book of the Samurai* Arms and Armour Press 1982

Turnbull, S.R. *Battles of the Japanese Samurai* Arms and Armour Press. In preparation

Varley, H.P. *The Onin War* Columbia University 1967

Index and Glossary

ILLUSTRATIONS
All the black and white photographs used in this book are by the author, except for p. 114, the *wakizashi*, which was supplied by courtesy of Christie's.

All the colour plates, line illustrations and maps were specially prepared by James Field; the maps were annotated by Chartwell Illustrators. The author would like to thank the following individuals and organisations who gave permission for works in their possession to be photographed: Mr. I. Bottomley; Mr. T. Watanabe; the Nampian Kannon-ji, Kawachi-Nagano; Fudo-ji, Kurikara.

Samurai Warriors is an authoritative and vivid account of the costume and equipment of the Japanese samurai, and the development that came from changes in military history. Until the publication of this book non-Japanese-speaking readers had been denied accounts such as those produced by scholars like Yoshihiko Sasama. Several of Sasama's indispensable works, especially his *Zukai Nihon katchu jiten* (1973) and *Zuroku Nihon no katchu bugu jiten* (1981) have been consulted initially on points of detail for this work, but in every case the resulting illustration or description has been taken from source, making *Samurai Warriors* totally original.

It draws upon Stephen Turnbull's twenty years of research into samurai history, armour and weapons; and using his exclusively Japanese sources, paints a picture of the samurai in words and photographs. The addition of James Field's magnificent, specially commissioned colour artwork makes a book that is unique.

Stephen Turnbull graduated from Cambridge. He learned to read and write Japanese at Sheffield and his first visit to Japan was a study tour in 1970. In 1986 he was invited to play the part of the samurai general, Baba Nobuharu, in the Shingenko Festival at Shimobe, the first foreigner to take part in such a re-enactment of Japan's samurai past.

James Field's work includes museum displays on the Norman Conquest, conservation posters, booklets and model-making for television documentaries.

ISBN 0-7137-2285

9 780713 722857

£8.95